Don't Burn Anyone at the Stake Today

and other lessons from history about living through an information crisis

NAOMI ALDERMAN

FIG TREE
an imprint of
PENGUIN BOOKS

FIG TREE

UK | USA | Canada | Ireland | Australia
India | New Zealand | South Africa

Fig Tree is part of the Penguin Random House group of companies
whose addresses can be found at global.penguinrandomhouse.com

Penguin Random House UK,
One Embassy Gardens, 8 Viaduct Gardens, London SW11 7BW

penguin.co.uk

First published 2025

004

Copyright © Naomi Alderman, 2025

The moral right of the author has been asserted

This book is an update of and expands on the radio series *The Third Information Crisis*,
originally commissioned for BBC Radio 4 and broadcast in 2024

On page 21, photograph of Phoenician text [2D6R51] is © Uwe Deffner/Alamy Stock Photo and
photograph of cuneiform text [H99R8N] is © Images & Stories/Alamy Stock Photo

Penguin Random House values and supports copyright.
Copyright fuels creativity, encourages diverse voices, promotes freedom
of expression and supports a vibrant culture. Thank you for purchasing
an authorized edition of this book and for respecting intellectual property
laws by not reproducing, scanning or distributing any part of it by any
means without permission. You are supporting authors and enabling
Penguin Random House to continue to publish books for everyone.
No part of this book may be used or reproduced in any manner for the
purpose of training artificial intelligence technologies or systems. In accordance
with Article 4(3) of the DSM Directive 2019/790, Penguin Random House
expressly reserves this work from the text and data mining exception

Set in 12.5/14.75 pt Garamond MT Std
Typeset by Six Red Marbles UK, Thetford, Norfolk
Printed and bound in Great Britain by Clays Ltd, Elcograf S.p.A.

The authorized representative in the EEA is Penguin Random House Ireland,
Morrison Chambers, 32 Nassau Street, Dublin D02 YH68

A CIP catalogue record for this book is available from the British Library

ISBN: 978–0–241–77763–3

Penguin Random House is committed to a sustainable future
for our business, our readers and our planet. This book is made from
Forest Stewardship Council® certified paper

Contents

1. the most useful thing — 1
2. the uli that never fades — 15
3. on forgetting, and the right to forget — 31
4. the box-pew effect — 41
5. the rise in utter nonsense — 55
6. mapping the inner world — 69
7. the idea of a library — 81
8. loneliness — 95
9. a fast machine — 111
10. all right, but what am I supposed to do about all this? — 121
11. a wonderful catastrophe — 137
12. an afterword: the thing I haven't talked about — 141

Notes — 149
Bibliography — 153
Acknowledgements — 161

the most useful thing

What is the most useful thing you could know about your own life?

That's a question with a lot of possible answers. In this book I am suggesting a general answer – something that we might all get some use out of knowing about our own lives. It is: the name of the era you're living through.

We all live in history. A lot of the problems that face us, and the opportunities that present themselves, are defined not by our own choices or even the specific place or government we're living under, but by the particular epoch of human events that our lives happen to coincide with.

Just for example: the Industrial Revolution presented opportunities for certain kinds of business success – it made some people very rich while others became very poor and exploited. If you'd known that was the name of your era, it would have given you a clue about what kinds of events to prepare for. If you'd known that your time would later be called the Reign of Terror, that would also have given you a useful warning. We can choose to resist our era, to go with it, to exploit it or try to retreat from it. But only when we know what it is.

So, in this book I'm suggesting a name for the era we're living through. It is: the Information Crisis. It's not a single moment, it's an epoch – we're in the middle of it already and if you're reading this book within a couple of decades of 2025 when I'm writing it, sorry, but this information crisis is going to be going on for the rest of our lives.

Even more importantly, I'm arguing that this is the third great information crisis that human beings have gone through. The previous two were the invention of writing, and the invention of the Gutenberg printing press. Digital communications technology is the third crisis. I think these prolonged crises aren't just neutral technical improvements. I think they change us psychologically, socially and emotionally in profound ways that simply cannot be reversed. And I suspect we can learn a huge amount from looking at the previous two crises – to understand what we're facing, how it's likely to feel, the way it's going to change us and what are the best ways through.

This is a kind of speculative historical project, I grant you. I can't know what's going to happen in the future. But the more I've looked at the transition from oral culture to literacy, and from handwriting to printing presses, the more I've seen the same patterns. The more what we're living through right now feels eerily familiar.

I'm about to make some pretty radical claims about what information crises do to us. But although I'm drawing some threads together, I'm not the first to point out these links. The writers Walter Ong and Eric Havelock have written about the changes in human consciousness after the invention of – particularly – phonetic script; that is, a script like the one we use in English today, where all the words can be sounded out just by seeing them written down.

The Axial Age was a time between the eighth and third

centuries BCE when many of our greatest religious and philosophical thinkers lived. It takes in, in the words of the historian Arnaldo Momigliano, 'the China of Confucius and Lao-Tse, the India of Buddha, the Iran of Zoroaster, the Palestine of the Prophets and the Greece of the Philosophers'. The Axial Age represented a massive leap in thinking where people began to be able to think *about* thinking, to consider the minds we live in. The Egyptologist Jan Assmann has suggested that the Axial Age was a 'media event' which would never have happened without the invention of writing. That is to say: it's been *300,000* years or so since modern *Homo sapiens* emerged; in that time there have probably been many wonderful, wise teachers, but if there was no writing, once they were gone their thoughts were quickly gone too. It's only in the last *3,000* years that anyone who hadn't *met* those wonderful teachers could read their words decades or even centuries after their death and become a follower. That couldn't have happened without writing.

The links between the invention of the printing press and the Reformation are also well known. The historians and thinkers Elizabeth Eisenstein, Neil Postman, Tom Holland, Diarmaid MacCulloch and Marshall McLuhan have all written about how the invention of print technology meant that ordinary people could do away with intermediaries and connect for themselves with the writings about one of those wonderful teachers – Jesus. One historian of the Reformation, Bernard Cottret, has written: 'It was not the Reformation that created a need to read Scripture, but the reading of Scripture that brought about . . . the Reformation.' That widespread reading of scripture was only made possible by the printing press.

And what does that all mean for us? What we can see from the last two information crises is that there are enormous leaps forward in knowledge and understanding . . . but also a period of intense instability. After the invention of writing, the Axial Age was filled with new beautiful ideas and new moralities. And there was also the possibility of new kinds of warfare, motivated at least as much by religious and philosophical differences, or different interpretations of texts, as by desire for new territory or property. After the invention of the printing press came the Enlightenment, an explosion of new scientific knowledge and discovery. But before that Europe plunged into the Reformation, the creation of new Protestant Christian churches which broke away from the Catholic Christian church, no longer accepted the authority of the Pope and believed that priests weren't necessary for people to have a direct relationship with God. Catholics and Protestants were at war for centuries, different countries took different sides, even families were divided. The violence of the Reformation led to the destruction of statues and other artworks and many institutions that had been working at least *adequately* well until then.

And, to get to the heart of the matter, the Reformation in Europe meant a lot of people got burned at the stake, or killed in other terrible ways. Burning at the stake certainly didn't *begin* with the printing press and the Reformation; it's a very ancient form of death-by-torture. But it did happen during European conflicts of Reformation.

Take Michael Servetus, a person one feels really led a very worthwhile life. Born in Spain in around 1511, he studied at the University of Paris, learned and wrote about a huge number of different subjects – Wikipedia lists 'mathematics, astronomy and meteorology, geography, human anatomy . . . jurisprudence, translation, poetry' – and was the first European to give an accurate account of how pulmonary circulation works. Caught up in the fervour of the Reformation, he ended up burned at the stake for heresy in Geneva, after being condemned by Luther and Calvin. Or take Peter Ramus, the inventor of the concept that you should write a textbook on any subject by proceeding first through more simple things and then to more complex things. He was a Protestant, killed by the mob in the St Bartholomew's Day Massacre in Paris in 1572.

Just to think for a brief moment about what 'burning at the stake' actually means: it's without doubt one of the worst things humans are capable of. In her book *The Burning Time*, Virginia Rounding describes the burnings that took place at Smithfield in London. 'Bundles of brushwood, rods and sticks' were tied together. The victim would be 'bound to the stake by chains'. There were onlookers: 'some sympathizers there to support the victims, others come to enjoy the spectacle – all waiting for the moment when the bodies, charred and melted by the flames, would topple over their chains and into the fire.' It could take a long time. Rounding writes that depending on the weather, on a rainy day the victim might die only after 'an hour of excruciating agony'. While the people around smelled 'the smoke, the scent of roasting human flesh'.

It is true but hard to really accept that the invention of the printing press led to hundreds of years of torture and bloodshed about what seem to many of us now very small doctrinal differences. Like whether the bread and the wine consumed during the Eucharist were *really* the body and blood of Christ or just a *symbol* of the body and blood of Christ. This is still a real difference between Catholics and Protestants.[1] But ways have been found – for the most part – to live and let live. For almost everyone the question about transubstantiation has nothing like that same emotional intensity any more.

Looking back, it is deeply shocking that burning at the stake and other murders and torture happened – not just once, but over and over again – when all participants claimed to be following Jesus of Nazareth, a man who'd said, reported in those printed books: 'love one another'.

I'm using 'burning at the stake' as a shorthand in this book – for all the things people end up doing in the throes of a doctrinal dispute that are really completely against the values they would otherwise claim to hold. They are things that involve turning a living, breathing person into a symbol, something that can be treated with extreme cruelty to make your point. When I talk about 'burning at the stake' I don't mean 'criticizing someone's views in mature debate' or 'protesting against government policies'. I mean the things that demean you as a human if you do them to others. I mean the point when the desire to *just win this argument* turns you into someone who goes against all your other values. There is never a good enough reason to burn someone at the stake.

I think the following is incontestable: trying to get rid of all opinions that are different to yours can only ever be attempted by unthinkably vast human rights atrocities. (And even then it doesn't actually work. There are still, in fact, both Catholics and Protestants.)

And I think we can already see the outlines of how this type of thing becomes more common during an information crisis because we're back in another one. We're all overloaded and overwhelmed by information. If you were born in the 1990s or earlier, the amount of information you can access now in a day compared to when you started secondary school is orders of magnitude larger. We live in a tidal wave of data, coming at us constantly. We don't have the social and informational structures in place yet to manage it.

My suggestion is that this enormous information wave makes us anxious and angry.

How? All this information introduces us to all the things we don't know, all the ways in which we're not experts. We might end up expressing an idea online which we've heard many times in our social circle only to be jumped on by fifty people who know more and tell us that our ideas are stupid, old-fashioned and even prejudiced. If this has ever happened to you – and it's happened to a lot of people – it can make you feel profoundly unsettled, frightened, out of touch. That might be a good thing. It's also an emotionally destabilizing thing. It works the other way around too. When we can see everyone else's opinions, it turns out that someone we really liked may hold an idea that we find stupid, old-fashioned or even prejudiced.

It's the 'I used to like Uncle Bob until I saw his posts on Facebook' syndrome. We're left wondering who we can trust and whether we're actually surrounded by upsetting idiots. This can all leave anyone feeling isolated and misunderstood, unsupported, frightened, worried and angry.

Well, that's probably very much how it felt in Reformation Europe to find out that your next-door neighbour had a very different idea to you about whether the bread and wine of the sacrament were really the body and blood of Christ.

Which is to say: we can expect this to get worse before it gets better.

It's important to explain at this point something that's going to come up again and again: there are two related but distinct changes that happen when these new technologies arise. One is mechanical and the other – the most important one – is psychological.

The mechanical change is quite easy to understand. There are obvious efficiencies of new information technologies which open up time and space for other work and which make things possible that just weren't possible before. If you don't have to memorize enormous amounts of text, you have more time and mental space available for reflecting on it. You just can do certain kinds of work and research much more quickly once writing exists. And again more quickly after printing exists. And much, much more quickly now the internet and indeed generative AI exist.

But I'm most interested in the *psychological* effects. The way the new technologies end up shaping how we think, how we feel, even what we're able to perceive.

An example of the difference is this: in the early sixteenth century, long before he nailed any theses to any door at Wittenberg, Martin Luther – the originator of the Reformation – had his own copy of the Bible printed. For centuries, Bibles had been hand-copied surrounded by commentaries or 'glosses' – as in 'a gloss on a text' – collected from the writings of early church fathers and later theologians. These commentaries might explain, note a related thought, make minor points about interesting etymologies of words or major points about the right way to interpret an idea. The historian Lesley Smith has written that a standard belief was: 'to read the Bible without the Gloss was to read a Bible which could not speak – or rather, one whose speech could not properly be understood.'

But Luther asked the university printer to print an edition of the Bible without any commentaries for him, so he could sit with the pure word of God. It was working on that text which resulted in the conclusions that led him to write his theses which, in the end, created Protestantism.

Before the invention of printing, anyone who wanted an edition of the Bible exactly to their specifications would have had to copy the entire Bible out by hand, or get someone else to do it. So printing opened up the possibility of owning one's own copy, printed in one's own way. It opened up time for deep thinking without the mental interruption of commentaries. That's mechanical change.

But the existence of printing also opened up a new attitude to the Bible. Thinkers like Marshall McLuhan might say that the possibility of easily reading a Bible with no intermediary suggests the new idea that a person's relationship with God needs no intermediary. That's *psychological* change.

This is what information crises do. They open up new ways of thinking. And for better or worse, we're in the middle of one right now.

This book isn't going to say that the internet is good, or bad. It's absolutely both, and we'll look at both. What we're trying to do is be prepared for the things that happen in every information crisis; even without technology billionaires pulling the strings. There are plenty of books which focus on the dangers posed by the values – and lack of values – of technology billionaires, and, to be clear, I think those dangers are real. But this book is mostly about what happens in an information crisis to all of us, about the kinds of risks and opportunities that exist. To understand what it might mean to mitigate the worst and leap towards the best. To recognize that we *already know* many of the values we need and how to act well during an information crisis. I'm going to look at the past to see what we can learn from it about the present and the future.

People really did burn each other at the stake. It was a horrific, diabolical act done in the name of God. The forces I'm talking about here are murderously strong.

I should say: this is not the only way to slice history. I've picked writing and the printing press because I think they are the most seismic shifts which are most analogous to the invention of the internet, but it's perfectly possible to tell this story including a series of information shocks like the invention of telegraphy, radio and television. Technology is also absolutely not the only thing going on in history; there are many other factors to understand. And the story of information crises isn't even the only story to tell about how technology changes the way we think. So many new technologies have changed us. We could talk about warfare and weapons-making and how they've changed the way we live. I could tell a history of how horse, steam and electric power have challenged our ideas about gender by making human physical strength less and less important, which has rearranged our assumptions about whether men are more important than women. Or I could talk about how the moving image has changed human dreaming. Or we could trace the effects of the Industrial Revolution and uniform machine-made consumer products on our perception of our own bodies which are organic, non-homogenous, lumpy, bumpy, smelly . . . normal. Those histories, and dozens more, are worth telling.

But this one – the history of how information systems change how we think – is happening *right now*. It's affecting everything else that's going on because it's about how we find out what's going on. This is the lens through which we see everything else. Understanding that lens, knowing the name of our own era, might be the most useful thing we could know about our whole lives.

the uli that never fades

In Chinua Achebe's novel *No Longer at Ease*, the main character Obi Okonkwo's father tries to explain the power of writing to his son in this way:

> Our women made black patterns on their bodies with the juice of the uli tree. It was beautiful, but it soon faded [. . .] But sometimes our elders spoke about uli that never faded, although no one had ever seen it. We see it today in the writing of the white man. If you go to the native court and look at the books which clerks wrote twenty years ago [. . .] they are still as they wrote them [. . .] Okoye in the book today cannot become Okonkwo tomorrow [. . .] It is uli that never fades.

Writing is an extremely powerful technology, one of the most powerful that humans have ever invented. For Obi, writing is both his great strength and his terrible undoing. He is highly educated, works hard and has exceptional ambition but because of the financial system around him he becomes bound up in debts which he can't escape. The uli that never fades ends up written on him: as unbreakable as physical chains.

It is hard for us now, in a culture built on literacy, to really experience how writing shapes so many aspects of our world. But permanence is a big one. Like the modern internet, the invention of writing was a process which removed a previous 'right to forget and be forgotten'.

Before the invention of writing, there was – in a very real sense – no such thing as history. Things happened, of course, but the only way to record them was in memory via chants and stories, and perhaps in cave paintings and other art. And memory is intensely slippery – as anyone who's ever tried to reconstruct a conversation the next day knows. And if you don't know what a painting depicts after a few decades, or centuries at most, it becomes an intriguing set of figures whose meaning can only be guessed at.

The power of writing technology is almost impossible to overstate. As Obi Okonkwo discovers, it invents the concept of inescapable debt – it also makes possible advanced forms of trade, stock-keeping and taxation, bureaucracy and wills that express a person's wishes after death. It also made new forms of conflict possible for the very first time.

It would be completely ridiculous for me to claim that writing, printing or digital technologies are the source of all human conflict or even a major factor in the existence of violent conflict between humans. Violence exists everywhere in the world of living things on this planet: species and individuals compete for reproductive and sexual partners and for resources like places to live, water and food. When that food consists of other living beings, conflict is absolutely inevitable. There were wars, fights and weapons before there was writing. There's some evidence that the increasing interest in living in a symbolic world – the world of symbols like written letters – has meant less violent physical conflict in the real world. Again, none of this is wholly good or wholly bad.

What we can say is that the symbolic world of written words, of printing and now of the internet, introduces the possibility of a *war of interpretation* – in which people fight ceaselessly about the meaning of maybe as little as a single written word or phrase. It creates conflict that goes on and on, because the words that were used remain fresh in writing as they never could in memory. And it creates the possibility of conflict with people you've never actually met.

The ancient Sumerians invented cuneiform – the earliest-known writing system in the world. They had a legend about how writing came to be invented. It was an argument between kings: King Enmerkar of Uruk and the Lord of Aratta. The Sumerian legend is that King Enmerkar was trying to send long messages of boasts and threats to the Lord of Aratta but the messages got *so* long that the messenger – who had to run there and back – kept forgetting important parts of the speech. So Enmerkar invented a system where he could make marks into a tablet of clay which was then baked hard in the sun. That way, the precise words of his insults could be conveyed to the Lord of Aratta.

Well, it's taken several thousand years to get here but now all of us can instantly send an insulting message to pretty much any king we want.

The story about King Enmerkar and the Lord of

Aratta is a legend, but many of the actual words sent by ancient Sumerians after the invention of writing can feel surprisingly modern. Cuneiform was originally mostly used for trade and record-keeping, making a careful account of how many goats or sheep someone had, how much grain was in a storehouse, or what quality of copper ingots you'd received. The famous complaint tablet to Ea-nāṣir is a customer complaint sent in around 1750 BCE. It's become an internet meme because it feels so intensely familiar. A. Leo Oppenheim translated the text this way in his really very entertaining book *Letters from Mesopotamia*:

> You did not do what you promised me. You put ingots which were not good before my messenger (Sit-Sin) and said: 'If you want to take them, take them; if you do not want to take them, go away!'
>
> What do you take me for, that you treat somebody like me with such contempt? I have sent as messengers gentlemen like ourselves to collect the bag with my money (deposited with you) but you have treated me with contempt by sending them back to me empty-handed several times, and that through enemy territory. Is there anyone among the merchants who trade with Telmun who has treated me in this way?

It goes on for quite a while and feels . . . well, the world seems full now of people shouting contemptuously at others that they shouldn't treat them with such contempt.

And cuneiform was just the start of it. The writers of that early writing system were mostly professional 'tablet-writers', because cuneiform was complex and difficult to learn. Early cuneiform was not phonetic – like the kind of script we use to write English, where every letter has a specific sound associated with it – but instead pictographic. You had to learn a different symbol for each word, so that's about a thousand different symbols. That demands time and concentration, and most people didn't have that amount of time in ancient Sumeria.

But phonetic script – the Phoenician alphabet invented about 3,000 years ago – was simple enough for almost anyone to learn. Instead of a thousand symbols to learn, you just needed to know about twenty. As we know now, almost everyone is capable of doing that. You didn't even have to have someone around who spoke a language to be able to sound out phonetic script. It was the equivalent of taking computers out of enormous rooms installed

Cuneiform carved scriptures at the National Museum of Iran, Tehran

A stele depicting King Kilamuwa from the Kingdom of Sam'al with a sixteen-line Phoenician text, Pergamon Museum, Berlin

by IBM and making them small enough for any of us to hold in our hand and carry with us. A technology that had been used just by a small rich elite became accessible to everyone. And it changed society.

Walter Ong was a thinker who devoted much of his career to understanding what happens to a culture when it transitions from orality to literacy. (I should note that everything I'm writing about here also applies to sign languages, which are still 'oral' languages in this sense rather than written ones.) Some of Ong's conclusions about that transition from oral to literate culture might be quite surprising.

For example: literacy, and especially phonetic script, causes societies to value elderly people less. Why? Let's look at the mechanical change first. Before literacy, societies need their older people desperately. They are the ones who can remember, let's say forty years ago, where was the safe place to shelter from the flood water the last time the river burst its banks? Being able to write that information down is certainly less risky. Information can be moved out of people's heads and into rock, papyrus or paper storage systems. But then you don't need the old people so much any more. Nor do you need to sit and listen to their stories of the olden days when you can read accounts of events written fresh, just after they happened. The psychological change in societies that rests on this mechanical change is that increasingly 'respect for the elderly' tends to become less common.

We're used to thinking about literacy as an unalloyed good – everyone wants more literacy! And there are tremendous benefits. But Ong says we need to recognize what literacy took away from us too. He says that literacy makes oral cultures less warm, less flexible, less personally interactive, less fundamentally *human*.

There's a theme here that's going to be repeated when thinking about how information technologies change societal values – once we can record what people think and distribute it easily, we need the actual people quite a bit less. As Ong wrote: 'Writing, and even more, print, downgrade the figures of the wise old man and the wise old woman, repeaters of the past, in favour of younger discoverers of something new.'

By this account, the idea that culture and society should above all be seeking what's new is invented by writing. Then it's pushed forward even more by printing, and even more so right now by the internet. Ong points out that in oral cultures a huge amount of time every day is spent repeating things that would otherwise fall out of memory – that might be sayings, aphorisms, songs, chants, poems, all the ways that we have of keeping things in our collective memories. It's widely accepted now, for example, that Homer's *Odyssey* and *Iliad* were products of an oral tradition of wandering bards who probably assembled the story – around key poles and moments, passages that were so well known that they would barely change – afresh each time they sung the poem. They were part of a cycle of works that included epic poems that are now completely lost or only exist as fragments, such as the *Titanomakhia* – the Battle of the Titans – or the *Cypria* – about the events leading up to the Trojan War. The legend is that Pisistratus, the ruler of Athens in around 559 BCE, commissioned a written copy of the *Odyssey* and the *Iliad*, turning those works of oral culture into artefacts of the world of writing.[2] Of course, the ability to write texts down did eventually mean that the oral transmission of text faded away and those other works were lost.

In an oral culture, text is only kept alive if it is in constant circulation and repetition. This means that oral cultures are essentially conservative. There are tricks by which memories can be made to work extremely accurately – think of how much easier it is to remember a set of words if you know they rhyme and fall into a meter. But it all takes time and there are limits.

Ong wrote that in oral cultures 'exploratory thinking is not unknown, but it is relatively rare' – he called it a 'luxury' because almost everyone has to spend the vast majority of their time – as he puts it – repeating 'the truths that have come down from the ancestors. Otherwise these truths will escape and culture will be back on square one.' It's the ability to write things down that makes culture speed up, to the pace of innovation we see today.

Ong's insight that people in literate cultures simply have more time for independent thinking than people in oral cultures suggests that after the invention of phonetic script many people who would otherwise have been rehearsing and repeating traditional songs, genealogies, poems and sayings would have had time to themselves to ponder new ideas.

The Axial Age was the long period of human history when enormous religious and philosophical figures like

Buddha, Moses, the Greek philosophers and Confucius emerged. It lasted for about 500 years and began just about 2,800 years ago – that is, just after writing became widespread. Arnaldo Momigliano wrote that everywhere the Axial Age happened, societies became interested in 'greater purity, greater justice ... and a more universal explanation of things' and in 'new models of reality'. That feels fairly familiar – we're back in another era when people are almost obsessively engaged in questions around purity, justice and the explanation of why things happen, whether that's a conspiracy theory or an idea about how society is structured. The historian Robert Bellah argues that – along with iron and the development of stronger weapons – development of a writing which most people could learn was one of the two key technologies that caused the Axial Age to happen. Bellah suggests that what was special about this epoch of history was that people began to experience 'theoretic culture' and 'second-order thinking' – that is, thinking about thinking – and that this could only happen because of the 'external memory' provided by writing. Once you can get your thoughts on paper you can look at them, as it were, from the outside. That's why journalling, or writing an essay, or jotting down some notes or a mind-map about a new project 'works'. You begin to be able to spot patterns in your own thinking, ways in which you go in circles or that what you're saying is self-contradictory. These are incredibly powerful mechanical changes which give an immense array of new tools to human thinking.

But there's also the psychological explanation. The

invention of a new technology as powerful as writing, the relative lack of need for old people, might make people think that actually new things are more valuable than old. Once a phonetic script is invented that most people can learn pretty easily, old hierarchical structures are easier to question. If you don't need to go to a scribe at the temple or the palace to get things written down, you might start to think things like: 'Maybe I am just like the King, at least in this way.' That thought in itself might leave you more receptive to ideas like the samsara cycle of reincarnation, in which the soul that inhabits you may have been both a king and an ant in the past. Or ideas like ancient Greek democracy. Or the Golden Rule of Hillel, where you can work out what the right thing to do is by asking yourself: 'Would I like it if someone else did that to me? If not, don't do it.' That's a real feeling of levelling which we can also see in the world today. A teenager and a billionaire can all use the same model of iPhone, the same WhatsApp or Instagram – there isn't a special Snapchat for the super-wealthy. Does that make it easier to question authority and old ways of doing things?

Inspired by the classicist Eric Havelock and the thinker Marshall McLuhan, I might go further than that. What do you think of this idea? If you work all day long with any technology it imprints itself on your mind. When people worked all day with sheep, they imagined God as a shepherd and humans as his flock. These days, working all day with computers, we talk about ourselves as brains that can be 'hard-wired' or 'programmed'. And what if the new technology you're spending your time with is phonetic script ... about twenty little symbols of the same size which can be ordered and reordered but always remain uniform and none is more important than the other? A script in which each symbol represents not ideas of kings and enslaved people but sounds, with no defining hierarchy. Might not the encounter with that technology tend your mind to think things like: 'We're all like the letters, we're all needed, we are all the same size, there is no one chief letter that is always at the front.' Which could incline you to think of people as somehow fundamentally more equal?

Well, you might find that fanciful. We can't know. We can only guess, moving our minds backward and forward in time, trying to use the present to explain the past and the past to explain the present.

As far as we can tell, there are extraordinary changes in morality after the invention of writing. I think we might be able to detect the traces of something similar happening now. Voices have a new and fundamental equality online. And even more so, now that we can see and hear through so many people's cameras around the world. Amateur shaky real videos of police brutality or the atrocities of war are very different to a dry newspaper paragraph or even a video package in a news programme. They come to us with an immediacy and clarity which makes it feel obvious that all human beings can suffer equally and deserve equal concern. This is not to say that all people instantly become very *good* – I don't think anything's going to do that to us, certainly not a technology. I'm arguing that these technologies refine our idea of what *good* is, encourage us to think that being good might mean giving equal concern to all people, ceasing to think of ourselves and our group as innately superior and our own needs as the paramount concern in the world. That is a hard definition of the good, and we're never going to live up to it. But I think it takes some of its force from writing which – as Walter Ong says – separates the speaker from what is said. You can be moved and changed by someone's words without ever having met them. So the most critical people in the world *can't* just be people we've met, in our own small circle.

This is also important: there is something fundamentally *uncanny* about writing. By which I mean: unsettling. A bit *weird*. Writing enables people to speak after they're dead, in their own precise words. That's a bit weird. Writing is unresponsive – you can argue with it as much as you like but it still goes on saying the same old thing. That's also really odd. Writing is a non-human object – a papyrus, a codex, now a phone made of glass and silicon – that pretends to be a human. Dealing with writing, I'd suggest, makes us profoundly unsettled in ways we might not always be aware of. And as with so many features of these technologies, the effects are paradoxical. At the same time that the information crisis encourages us to feel each other's humanity more deeply, it also brings into question whether our interactions via technology are with a human at all. When someone insults me online, am I dealing with a *person* – who I could expect to respond to my shock and distress with some degree of compassion – or am I dealing with an *object* which has no feelings and which I can just put down and walk away from without it deserving my respect or attention? This is even more true since the arrival of AI, of course, when the words I'm reading and the photo I'm seeing might not be a real person at all but just a computer program whose feelings I definitely can't hurt. That is disturbing. It tempts us to treat people online as if they might be disposable unfeeling computer creations, even if they really are people. Online dating, for example, can come to seem a game of swiping, scrolling and ghosting. We behave that way online, we are treated that way ourselves – in all sorts of contexts.

These unsettling questions and behaviours originate in writing. We still don't have good instincts about how to navigate them. We end up treated poorly online by people who think of us as somehow less than human. It makes us feel anxious, uneasy and distressed. We are more likely to act aggressively. And when we fear others' aggression, we lash out.

In our literate culture, we tend to think of both writing and reading as fundamentally peaceful activities that are 'good for us'. And that's also true. It's always both, never either/or.

What happens in an information crisis is that we have to deal with vastly more symbols than ever before. Our symbols speak to us as if they were people. A clay tablet brings us wonderful news, or insults us. Some ink on paper berates us, or tells us we're extraordinary. A block of glass and metal gets us to fall in love with it and then stops talking. What happens fundamentally is a confusion between people and symbols.

In an information crisis, because you're learning to treat more and more symbols as if they were people, it's easier to treat people as if they were symbols. That's where it's tricky. And because of the permanence of writing, while this is something we might get better at dealing with, it's a problem that's not going away.

on forgetting, and the right to forget

Quite a lot has been written already on the right to be forgotten. There are good reasons for this. Every information crisis has made it harder and harder for our past selves to be forgotten. And we've all done incredibly stupid things in the past, especially when we were young. We did something idiotic, we wore a stupid costume, we said an outrageous thing, we were generally objectionable. But time has moved on and we ought to have the right for that past version of us not to be dragged along with us into adult life.

This idea is now pretty uncontentious, even though it is difficult to implement. The data protection laws in the EU are an attempt to give everyone the right to have information about themselves taken down from the internet.

I would suggest that something potentially equally important is the right not just to be forgotten but to forget. To allow ourselves to move on internally.

Ted Chiang, the brilliant science-fiction writer and observer of technology, has written an excellent story on the nature of forgetting and how the technology of writing interferes with it. The story is called *The Truth of Fact, The Truth of Feeling*; like all his work it's short and hugely thought-provoking: please do read it.

It's a story that combines both a fictionalized version

of history and a fictional technology from the future. The future tech is called RemRem – a perfect form of memory in which everyone's life is always constantly recorded so that it's easy to check who really said what in an argument or conversation. The fictionalized history is that of a conflict within the Tiv people in 1941 – in what is now Nigeria – over a complicated question of heredity and succession. The story traces the outline of something that really did happen when oral cultures were brought into contact with literacy, often through the British Empire: the discovery that oral memory says one thing, but the written word says something else.

Oral culture is flexible. If the 'rightful king' of a particular region turns out to be an absolute fool or monster, the oral tradition of succession can easily be 'found' to be mistaken; memories change. But if the genealogies have been written down, you're going to have to deal with that fool/monster becoming king; there's very little way out of it apart from a full-on revolution.

In the story, Chiang differentiates between truth as 'precision' and truth as 'what is right for the community'. He writes: 'The idea that accounts of the past shouldn't change is a product of literate cultures' reverence for the written word. Anthropologists will tell you that oral cultures understand the past differently: for them, their histories don't need to be accurate so much as they need to validate the community's understanding of itself. So it wouldn't be correct to say that their histories are unreliable; their histories do what they need to do.'

This story is a way of thinking about what might be

happening to us psychologically when we encounter previous versions of ourselves via the internet. The technology Chiang invented – RemRem – is already beginning to exist in our world. People drive around with always-on dashcams to record what happens in the road around them. This is very useful when it comes to an insurance claim, or to preventing theft. (Again, none of this is ever either completely good or completely bad.) And the sheer amount of information that is available about us online has started to constitute a sort of diary.

There was a time, before the invention of writing, when the only way to encounter a previous version of ourselves was through our own memory or through others' memories. Memory is malleable; it softens some elements, it leaves others out entirely. Memory is one of Walter Ong's human, flexible, warm oral-culture systems. The imperfect way that our memory works mitigates against lasting conflict, for most of us, most of the time. Memories fade. When people say 'time heals', part of what they mean is that in memory things become less sharp and therefore less wounding. Even if the wound was very painful at the time, most of us don't have brains that can hold on to it in that wounding form for ever. Eventually, for most of us, it becomes very hard to hold in the memory precisely what it was that someone else said that really annoyed us or made us feel belittled or upset.

Writing, of course, changed that. Even reading your own teenage diary, even reading a diary from last year, it is very easy to be convinced that you know what happened in the past and then to be very surprised when confronted with absolute evidence that what you remembered was not, in fact, what happened. Written words don't fade or soften like memories. Words written down hundreds or even thousands of years ago can still be wounding not just emotionally but even physically. Martin Luther – the originator of the Reformation – wrote that Jews should be hounded out, that Jewish synagogues and schools should be burned.[3] There'd have been no way for his words to be remembered so perfectly as to be this distressing without writing. And without printing they wouldn't have travelled as far or as widely as they did. One of the consequences of printing, then, is the preservation and dissemination of thinking that was pretty foundational to the Holocaust.

As ever, there is no good and bad in this technology. Writing and printing are the same technology that allows us to read wise thoughts from antiquity, to learn from scientific observations made by Aristotle or Copernicus. It's a technology of remembering. It's neutral about what precisely is remembered.

What I'm considering here is the question of how much good work internally is done for us by the process of forgetting who we used to be, and who others used to be. This is what Ted Chiang's story is also about: the vital psychological importance of being able to simply forget who we used to be. And the important possibilities of growth that may come from being able to revisit who we used to be. In Chiang's story the protagonist also has a vital moment of insight by being able to revisit a long-ago argument via RemRem and see that he wasn't as reasonable and innocent as he'd remembered.

There is a way of attacking people now, which is to go through every post we can find that was ever made by that person in any public social media platform and to find the worst or most objectionable thing they have ever said and bring it to attention.

This has become a major problem since the start of the 2020s because now we are more than twenty years on from the massive internet boom of the 2000s. Twenty years is a long time – long enough for most of us to have changed our ideas on a lot of key points, for us to have been exposed to a range of different ideas, for us to have had a lot of different experiences. Twenty years turns a shitposting fifteen-year-old into a responsible thirty-five-year-old.

Twenty years is long enough to grow up.

Twenty years is long enough to find that you don't really recognize the person you were before.

It used to be that we might be confronted with our young selves through our own personal diaries. Only public figures who knew themselves to be speaking to a mass audience – and who were probably working with an editor or a producer to shape what they said – would have been able to have their words or speech from twenty years earlier thrown back at them in public.

That's not the case any longer. Perfect technological memories give us information about ourselves we couldn't have found out in previous generations. Photography has enabled – or forced – us all to confront the minute changes in our faces year by year, decade by decade. In a time of portrait-painting, or with the best looking glasses available, no one would have been able to hold up a perfect image of their face from a few years earlier next to their own face and see precisely which wrinkles were new, see exactly the changes in the shape of cheeks or lips. We knew we were getting older, but the details were indistinct. I can't say that this has *caused* some new kind of obsession with how we look – people have always cared about how they look and some form of cosmetics and body-painting has been part of a huge number of cultures around the world. I do find it interesting, though, that constant availability of instant photography has coincided with an increasing ubiquity of 'tweakments' designed to address those minute wrinkles which are almost imperceptible unless you're looking at two photos side by side.

Similarly, I think it is unsettling to encounter a previous version of your own ideas and beliefs. Unsettling perhaps in the same way that it can be to hear a recording of your own voice or see a video of yourself from an unusual angle. It causes what psychologists call 'cognitive dissonance' – the sense that the image of the world you have inside your head is at odds with the world as it is. People will go to great lengths to resolve cognitive dissonance, because it feels so uncomfortable.

I think there probably is a condition or an experience which I'd call – in a tongue-in-cheek way – 'internet poisoning' or 'internet toxicity'. One can sometimes see this happening to celebrities and people with large social media followings. Perhaps someone is angry with them and trawls through twenty or more years' worth of their information and thoughts and confronts them with something which now sounds racist, sexist or homophobic.

The conversation moves very quickly. There is a great deal of anger and defensiveness. The person under attack may end up 'doubling down' on that previous version of themselves which in other circumstances they would have been able to forget. There is a maddening quality to having to be perfectly identical to a previous version of yourself – both in the way you look and in the views you hold.

Living as we are through an information crisis, when we're going to be confronted with an exponentially larger amount of new facts, opinions and ideas, it is even more important to accept that our ideas will change – sometimes very quickly. But of course, paradoxically, living through this information crisis means that we will be confronted with our own past ideas and selves – and the past ideas and selves of others – much more often, much more vividly than was possible even twenty years ago. The #MeToo movement, for example, changed a lot of minds simply by prompting women to share their own experiences of harassment and assault. When we read these stories and think about them, it would be actively strange for our ideas not to change.

Where does this leave us? We need to find ways to say 'I am not that person any more' and to account for it. 'I am not that person any more because I have thought again about this.' 'I am not that person any more because I have seen and understood new testimony and come face to face with new experiences.' It should be unsurprising now that many people have seen more than they could see before and have changed their minds. We should not be surprised that we don't look like a photograph of ourselves at twenty. We shouldn't be surprised that it's difficult to accept that we've changed that much either.

One reason all this is especially tough is what I'll discuss in the next chapter under the name 'the box-pew effect'. Our communications technologies encourage us to turn to them rather than to each other to find out anything, including who we are. Instead of looking at other human faces to understand ourselves in relationship to them, we're increasingly stuck in box pews, looking straight at our phones, asking them to tell us about ourselves.

the box-pew effect

In around 1440, in Mainz, Germany, Johannes Gutenberg came up with the movable-type printing press. Compared to what had come before – hand-copying and woodblock or metal plates – it was an extraordinarily quick and efficient way of reproducing texts.

Previously in Europe printing had been done via creating a whole metal- or wooden-plate image of the entire page, carving each letter by hand. There had been forms of movable type in China and Korea, where each character was created as a separate small block that could be moved around – which was much less time-consuming. But those were forms of writing which had a large number of characters. It was the combination of movable type – a small metal piece representing each letter – *with languages written in phonetic script*, where only about twenty-five individual pieces are needed, which was revolutionary. In movable type, each small block is a letter. You line them up in a frame to make words, with pieces of plain metal – strips of lead often, also called leading – between the words and lines to make gaps. This can be done so much more quickly than carving the page by hand. My mother worked as a graphic designer in the 1960s and 1970s and told me about typesetters laying out a whole newspaper page accurately in a few minutes, their fingers moving to put each letter in the right place faster than she could follow. What had been a hand-crafted, lengthy, expensive process became relatively rapid, easy and affordable.

After Gutenberg's invention, the number of books available to the ordinary person increased massively. It became possible for large numbers of people to own their own copies of the Bible and study it privately. This was a slow change, by our standards – literacy was still very low. But within eighty years, Martin Luther would be coming to his own personal understanding of the Bible, and his ninety-five theses criticizing the Catholic church would be printed, translated and read across Europe. The increase in Bibles created the Reformation. Like the Axial Age, the Reformation was a media event.

It's actually impossible to list all of the parallels between our current era and the Reformation. Tom Holland, author of the brilliant history of Christianity *Dominion*, has pointed up some of the similarities. In the Protestant Reformation, people toppled statues, argued viciously, murderously about transubstantiation and often came to believe that there was no point trying to do anything about the great problems of the world, because 'works' were unimportant compared to having good thoughts. Well, that all feels quite familiar. The Protestant Reformation called for ordinary people to develop their own personal relationship with God without intermediaries. The internet revolution has produced calls for 'disintermediation' in all areas of life, whether it be summoning your own taxi via an app, booking your own flights without a travel agent, getting rid of gatekeepers to publication and broadcast, or doing your own research about Covid and vaccines and not relying on experts.

During the Reformation, institutions that had been working adequately and doing useful functions for many people over centuries – like the monasteries and convents – were suddenly swept up in a rush to condemn their failings. Monasteries weren't perfect by any means. Some of them *were* corrupt, self-serving and even abusive. But they'd also been doing the very valuable work of almsgiving, tending to the sick, providing a bed for the night for the very poorest. And convents had been centres for women's education, something that was then blocked for centuries. It was only after the Dissolution of the Monasteries that England had to institute laws about vagrancy. Today, as we go through our third information crisis, many long-standing institutions are similarly finding themselves under threat because of their perceived lack of various kinds of perfection.

How did this all happen in the Reformation? First of all, there was a mechanical change. Diarmaid MacCulloch, in his book *Reformation: Europe's House Divided*, has written: 'Before the invention of printing, a major part of a scholar's life was spent copying existing texts by hand, simply in order to have access to them. Now that printed copies of texts were increasingly available, there was less copying to do, and so there was more time to devote to thinking for oneself.' That's very familiar – it's just so much easier now to read and research almost anything. That's part of the way I've been able to write this book. I can access many books online, download them, I don't need to get myself to a library or trawl through a microfiche catalogue. It's just faster, so there's more time for more thinking work.

And then there was the psychological change. MacCulloch says that the central place of 'copying' before Gutenberg had made people feel that ancient knowledge was more important than 'original thought'. Once your days aren't all spent copying – or searching library microfiche – the same idea occurs as with the invention of writing. Maybe old thoughts aren't important? Maybe brand-new thoughts are the best ones? I'd suggest that that's where the current drive to disintermediate, the technology company mantra of 'move fast and break things', comes from too.

And, as we saw with the development of literacy, reading fosters individualism. It gives us more space and time for our own thoughts, and turns us from being mostly part of a community to being mostly individuals, with our own individual ideas, thoughts and relationships. MacCulloch has also written about how, in the years 1490 to 1517, as printed books became increasingly common, this individualism became clear in the very fabric of churches. He explains that as it became easier to acquire a 'printed layfolk's companion to the Mass, or a Book of Hours', it became more normal for laypeople to think of the pious life as involving long deep hours of reading and reflection – rather than focusing mostly on communal prayer and listening to sermons. At this point, the presence of other worshippers started to seem a distraction from the true relationship with God, and wealthy people began to build 'enclosed private pew[s]' so that they could concentrate more fully on their own individual experience of prayer. Once we're able to access more information for ourselves – whether it's through having our own printed holy books or fast broadband at home – we start to trust ourselves, and focus on ourselves in a new way. That is wonderful and satisfying. And it is inevitably going to lead to conflict, once we're all coming up with our own personal truths.

That deep engagement with sources, I suspect, also creates a vulnerability to a very particular rigid kind of fundamentalism. As we've already seen, Walter Ong, the scholar of orality and literacy, reminds us that one of the key problems of literacy is that *people* can change as we interrogate their ideas but texts can't. Of course, written sources are incredibly valuable. They tell us things we couldn't learn any other way. But their very *value* leads us to prioritize the way writing works – with an increased feeling that it's somehow admirable or better *not to change or modify your view* and certainly not in response to disagreement. Those people in the closed-off pews not only can't see how others are reacting to a certain prayer, they're uninterested in finding out, they believe it's better not to know. The phenomenon of the 'internet bubble' is part of this. I have absolutely seen people on social media saying that it's actually better not to seek out alternative information, or try to talk to people who disagree with you. I've seen this from all sides of the political spectrum. It can certainly lead to increased concentration and focus – one of the glorious things about the modern internet is how deeply knowledgeable it's possible to become about anything from quantum theory to pop culture. If you want to do a 'deep dive' into a topic, the internet will go as deeply as you want, and introduce you to the opinions of thousands who are as interested as you are in the question of which is the best hotel in Rotterdam, or what barbecue cleaning brush to buy. We can focus with others who care about what we care about. And that means we can also shut out anything that distracts us, even if what's distracting about it is that it happens to be the truth.

There are certainly many people who have been dragged into entirely false conspiracy theories or cult-like online belief systems or quack ideas dressed up to look like legitimate scientific research. So the move towards individualism can paradoxically lead to the formation of more rigid think-alike communities.

There was a passionate feeling in the Reformation about returning to some earlier, better state of thinking, closer to the origin and pure root. When Luther had his Bible printed without commentaries, he believed himself to be seeking the pure word of God. But of course, seeking the pure word *is* difficult with Scripture. So much is lost when words are written down: all of those elements of tone, context, voice, facial movements, eye contact. Most of it. No one can go back to Jesus and Hillel and ask them what they really meant and whether any of what got written down was, for example, a bit sarcastic. But everyone wanted to feel that their interpretation was the pure, true, original one.

Tom Holland and Dominic Sandbrook pointed out in their podcast *The Rest is History* that this is currently happening in two different directions in academia. Right-wing writers like Jordan Peterson call for a return to traditional values and the study of Shakespeare as a more pure root of education, something more essentially true. Meanwhile left-wing thinkers call for subjects to be 'decolonized'. Each in their own way is calling for a perceived 'taint' to be removed from learning, for it to become closer to what they think of as its true origins.

The great historian of the print revolution Elizabeth Eisenstein has an important insight about the search for pure truth in the Reformation. She argues that science took over from religion as the repository of truth when – among other things – the Danish astronomer Tycho Brahe 'confronted by conflicting astronomical tables' could 'check both versions against a "pure original" – against fresh observation of uncorrupted "writing in the sky"'. That is to say, Tycho Brahe saw that astronomical observations in ancient works were incorrect and started again from scratch.

Tycho Brahe lived from 1546 to 1601, so he was born a bit more than a hundred years after Gutenberg's invention of the printing press. In 1572, Brahe observed a 'new star' in a place where the writings at the time said there wasn't supposed to be a star; this was so shocking that he dedicated the rest of his life to making completely fresh observations of the heavens which became famous for their tremendous accuracy. For that accuracy of observation, Brahe has been credited with helping to launch the scientific revolution. It was by taking a brand-new look, and by insisting on scrupulous exactness, that Brahe found the truth. It just wasn't possible to do that with Scripture – there were too many competing versions of old documents. Arguably, the desire for truth eventually pushed the entire culture more and more into science rather than religion.

I do think that what we're living through now is another massive increase in the sincere pursuit of truth. It's common on the internet to accuse others of being insincere or 'performative' in their beliefs, to simply disbelieve people about what they say. But I think what's actually happening is that we're seeing so many different kinds of information that it's difficult to synthesize them into a single easy-to-explain 'truth' – it can be easy to disbelieve people if we haven't seen the precise things they've seen. There's a lot to see. As we've been able to access more direct windows into other lives – social media posts, livestreams, videos, written testimony – it has turned out that a lot of what we thought we knew about people was wrong. When we see body-camera videos of people walking down the street and experiencing racism, sexism, ableism, fat-prejudice or homophobia, we realize how many different lives are being lived in parallel with our own. This is what the interest in 'lived experience', in believing different groups about their own lives, in seeking out writing by 'own voices' is about. Like Tycho Brahe, we are trying to return to the 'pure original'. And we are discovering how many different truthful 'lived experiences' there are.

There's a push–pull here. Worrying about the truth causes people to seek out *more* truth, *purer* truth. But then the more truths are available the more overwhelming it becomes and the more attractive it is to hold on to just one of them and decide that, no, you don't need any more information. That's it. I have my truth and I'm sticking to it. I look for more people who agree with me on everything. If a single individual or a whole organization like a convent or a university or a newspaper has disagreed with me once, in any context, I condemn them root and branch.

Something important is going on. I think we need to perceive ourselves as *partway through* an enormous cognitive change. There was something genuinely amazing on the way after the Reformation. Tycho Brahe might have been the start of it. A revolution in seeking for truth led to a scientific revolution and the Enlightenment. In the Enlightenment, the ability to share information swiftly and accurately turned into the scientific method, the discoveries of important things like gravity. Electricity. And steam power. And calculus. And the principles of chemistry. And the way the human body works. Eventually the discoveries of science relegated religion from being the ruler of kings and the arbiter of truth to . . . something more nebulous about moral values and spiritual feelings. Not that those aren't important. But it was *that* cognitive change that eventually made it baffling that people had spent the early years of printing using it to argue about transubstantiation.

Here in the 2020s, we're not there yet. We're still in the phase of using the new information distribution system to argue about our past, about the old structures of power and how they distribute the shreds of influence they allow to escape their grasp. We can't really even imagine the new futures yet, the things that will come along that make the topics we're currently getting heated about look baffling. My strong prediction is that this new way of distributing information is going to create a new frame through which to view the world. And I don't know what it is. Which I find exciting.

Writer and thinker Neil Postman has described the social change that had to happen to get through the Reformation and into the Enlightenment. For one thing, we had to rewrite the idea of childhood: 'In 1480,' he writes, 'there were thirty-four schools in all of England. By 1660 there were 444, one school for every twelve square miles.' *Now*, there are more than 24,000 schools in England and we've gone from roughly one school for every 75,000 people to one school (and probably a much, much larger school) for about every 2,400 people.

That's an extraordinary change. To deal with the flow of information we had to take school from a very minority pursuit into something that every child does for the majority of their waking days for at least twelve years. We needed to invent the idea of a curriculum and the textbook; that is: ways to sift and condense enormous amounts of information. It began to be normal for a book to have a contents page, an index; for books to be catalogued in standard ways; for indexes and books to be arranged in alphabetical order. The system of peer review of papers for journals was invented, systems of journalistic ethics and safeguards on accuracy. The world of print eventually became something any ordinary person could learn to navigate, and with skills tell truth from falsehood, at least most of the time. Well. We're going to need some new institutions, ideas and ways of organizing to get us through this current information crisis, as well as making sure to preserve some older ideas and institutions for as long as we can.

The box-pew problem is in some ways a problem of social proof – seeking truth we turn towards this wonderful new technological source of information and away from other people. But with the new technology, sources of truth multiply. And without other people, how do we know which technological sources we can trust?

When I was fifteen years old, the system of trustworthiness and proof in print material was very well developed – as it turned out it was as well developed as it was ever going to get. It was very easy to have one's inane or insane ramblings photocopied thousands of times, but we had very mature structures to let us know which printed material was basically trustworthy, written by professionals, and which wasn't. Did you get it from a newsagent or a person handing things out on the street? Did it look professionally laid-out and typeset? Had someone you trusted told you this was a good source?

Those systems mostly don't exist yet for the internet; everything comes via the phone or computer, it's trivially easy to make things look professional. And as we turn from each other and towards our devices, we're leaning very heavily on social proof. That's why it feels so devastating when someone you thought you knew turns out to think something that seems to you at least ... utter nonsense.

the rise in utter nonsense

Some of the research for this book has been exciting and some of it has been terrifying. Often on the same page. In my copy of Elizabeth Eisenstein's seminal work on the effects of the printing press, *The Printing Revolution in Early Modern Europe*, I have written an expletive next to the following passage, because it struck me as so frighteningly explanatory and true of the world we're living in now:

> Certain confusing cross currents may be explained by noting that new links between disciplines were being forged before old ones had been severed [. . .] When 'technology went to press', so too did a vast backlog of occult lore, and few readers could discriminate between the two.

Well, *bugger*. Here we are, once again. Just as after the print revolution in early modern Europe, it is now massively easier to access scientific information. That is to say, Tycho Brahe's truth. In a few seconds I can find a video clearly explaining particle physics, chemical bonds or how vaccines work. And at the same time it is also extremely easy to find very plausible-looking information that is completely false about how vaccines are actually terrible and suggesting solutions that I really don't even want to write down here in case it adds to the oversupply of 'occult lore'. It turns out that quite a few readers can't discriminate between the two.

Here's a story from my own working life. Years ago, I was the Lead Writer of an 'alternate reality game' called Perplex City. It was a game that you played by solving puzzle cards that led you through a mystery set in that city; the city wasn't in our world, but the conceit of the storytelling was that we could read their websites. So you could follow along with the story, read blogs, look at websites from the university, the police department, websites for the apartment buildings, even pharmaceutical websites.

As part of the story, we invented a drug called Ceretin, which we said was a neuro-enhancer that you might take if you wanted to study better and get more work done. The drug was, just to be clear, completely fictional. There was no such thing. But we made a website for it, with some vital clues about the mystery for our players. All good clean fun.

Around that time we held a party for some of our most enthusiastic players. And we thought it'd be fun to get some M&Ms printed up with the brand name Ceretin on, just to have bowls of our fictional neuro-enhancing drug dotted around with the canapés. All very delightful. Except that the M&M company came back refusing to print the logo on the chocolates because ... they don't print the name of real drugs on their sweets.

That was a bit of a moment for all of us at that time, and I've never forgotten it. What those of us who worked on Perplex City understood was that we'd entered a different world, where the verification systems are different. It used to be that to be a plausible-looking business you had to have a physical address, an office you could invite people to, headed notepaper, business cards, probably a staff member answering a phone, a listing in the Yellow Pages (remember those?) or other similar business directories. It was still *possible* to create a fake business, of course – think of all the stuff they do in the movie *The Sting* to fake up a bookie's office. But it was a lot of work.

Making that fake website for Ceretin had taken a couple of hours and the purchase of some stock images. It'd be even easier now, obviously. I wouldn't even have to write the text; ChatGPT could do that and Dall-E could create the images of laughing young women next to salad, feeling so happy about the Ceretin they'd just taken.

The internet has made it so much easier in so many ways to create a real business, or pretty much any other creative project one can imagine. It's also much, much easier to create convincing fakes, in all sorts of ways. You actually need quite a lot of skill to tell the difference between the fake and the reality. It is often a specialized job. I am not really that surprised that not every reader can discriminate between the two.

At the time of writing, the United States secretary of health is Robert F. Kennedy Jr, a man who, according to BBC fact-checking, has repeated the debunked Wakefield claim that vaccines cause autism in children; believes that fluoridation of water causes IQ loss; and says that Covid-19 is targeted at Caucasians and black people, while 'the people who are most immune are Ashkenazi Jews'.

If that's not a post-Gutenberg Luther-style information-crisis thing to believe, I don't know what is. This is the person who is in charge of healthcare in the richest and most powerful nation on the planet. This is not just a minor problem, it is a serious problem and it is likely to get worse.

Facebook has decided to follow Twitter in not employing fact-checkers any longer but just having a system of 'community notes'. The problem with this is obviously that communities aren't experts – they can easily become think-alike box-pew-sheltered echo chambers – and they can end up sharing and amplifying more and more false information. The problem, to quote Eisenstein again, is really 'few readers could discriminate between the two'.

As ever, we are lucky to live in a world where some of these problems have been solved once already. Unlike people living through the print revolution, we do have sophisticated networks of trusted information-dispersal which are still fairly robust. It is possible to learn which ones to consult and how to do fact-checking. The BBC has a good fact-checking service. Snopes and PolitiFact are good fact-checking services. There are others, and it's worth getting familiar with them. Fact-checking *is* a specialized skill, though, and it is becoming more challenging as the fakes get ever more convincing.

Goodness knows, I have sometimes shared information on social media which turned out to be false. It's very embarrassing, and I feel the urge every time to double down on my mistake and claim that there is some way in which it sort of *is* true even though it's definitely not.

I am also in that group Eisenstein identifies of people who can't always discriminate between what is true and what I'd like to be true.

Something I try to do these days is to notice how something I want to share on social media is making me *feel*. If I have a very strong feeling of any type, I try to use that as a cue to slow down and check my facts. It could be a strong gleeful feeling of: 'Oh, this is rich.' Like one I saw today, a tweet claiming to be by Donald Trump from a few years ago, saying that if the Dow drops 1,000 points in a day, the President should be impeached. 'Oh, this is rich,' I thought to myself. And obviously, it's fake. Or if I feel 'Oh God, that's dreadful what those people are doing', that's also a good sign it might be fake. If it feels too perfectly tailored to me, if it presses my buttons, if it precisely tickles me where I like to be tickled or hurts me where I am vulnerable to being hurt, that's a sign to check whether it's fake.

Obviously the whole point about an information crisis is that it's going to keep happening, no matter what we do. But we're going to need some new social norms. I think that getting into the habit of pausing online whenever you feel a very strong emotion and a desire to repost is not a bad new norm to learn ourselves and teach children. Probably also some norms around what you do when you see someone sharing something false would be good too. Don't embarrass them in public. It's going to happen to you one day too. Think about how you'd like that person to approach you. A private note, where you're on their side. It is extremely easy to alienate people via text communication because of all the oral-culture things that are missing from text. 'Argh, that made me laugh so much but I don't think it's true?' Probably one of the ways that we get through this is by trying not to pointlessly alienate the other humans.

Another is to shore up the organizations we do have that are still fundamentally trying to uncover and disseminate the truth. I think we are going through a period of profound crisis in our sources of information for absolutely predictable reasons connected to the invention of new, revolutionary technologies. In times like this it becomes much, much easier for even complex societies to break down into war and destruction. Every protective factor is important.

Institutions that are sources of basically truthful information are going to be particularly vulnerable when, inevitably, they do get something wrong. There is no such thing as an information system which never gets anything wrong. What we're looking for is a rapid acknowledgement of the problem, lack of defensiveness, curiosity about how it happened, a focus on systems and not individuals as the way to make sure it doesn't happen like that again. That's the ideal.

Even with the ideal system, the nature of an information crisis is that there will be plenty of people willing to tear down a good-faith truth-seeking organization over errors, who will use an error or a bad member of that organization as evidence that nothing from that source can be trusted.

So, which institutions are we being tempted to condemn root and branch because of some mistakes and abuses? What organizations are we going to allow our rulers to condemn because we can now find out more about them than we used to and we're horrified by some of the bad stuff that is going on? What large, trying-to-be-helpful-but-sometimes-failing associations would various rulers like to break up and destroy because it represents an alternative source of authority to their own narrative and also there's money to be made?

This is going to be different in different countries.

I think in the UK, it's the BBC.

I want to suggest that as British people we need to understand how valuable and important the BBC is in protecting us against the worst of the information crisis, how many forces want to tear it down, and how we will never get those protections back again if we allow it to be destroyed.

The BBC is not perfect. No organization of that size ever could be. It employs somewhere around 20,000 people and inevitably some of them are going to make mistakes or just be bad at their jobs. The BBC has made some terrible errors, both in its reporting of news stories, and in its employment and promotion of some people who were bullies or actual abusers. The BBC's role in keeping Jimmy Savile in the public eye, in giving him a platform to present himself very specifically as the best friend to all children and the one who could make all their dreams come true is . . . it's just horrific. It's upsetting, it's disgraceful, it's nauseating.

If you think about programming that is important to you or a subject on which you're an expert, you can probably think of something just laughably false or extremely bad that the BBC has broadcast about it. To take a minor example, I remember an academic talking on some radio programme about 'the Judaeo-Christian idea of everlasting hell' which . . . well, Jews don't believe in everlasting hell, so that was just stupid. No one challenged it. The BBC does this sort of thing all of the time.

I am not defending specific actions of particular producers or broadcasters, nor an individual stupid view I've heard on the BBC, nor abusers, nor bullies. It is a defence of the *principle* that the knowledge and media landscape is vitally important to the intellectual, educational, informational health of the nation, and that there should be a publicly funded organization dedicated to caring for that landscape. That it should be dedicated to producing true information, in an interesting way, and to curating media for us that is both entertaining and educational. The Reithian principle – inform, educate and entertain – is a good one.

It's not that complicated, actually. It is the same as the way British people defend the NHS. We aren't defending Harold Shipman and the vile, despicable murders he committed. We're not speaking up for the Alder Hey scandal, where body parts from hundreds of infants were retained without consent. We're not defending people being left in corridors all night in pain, or long waiting lists or supercilious doctors or botched operations or bad leaflets or stupid refusal of needed prescriptions. We're defending the principle. Healthcare, free at the point of use, for everyone.

I don't excuse any organization that harbours abusers; there are things that can be done to safeguard, and the presence of abuse is always a sign that there have been large institutional failures. I think it's also worth remembering that abusers and predators want to take advantage of the halo of trust in places where there is access to vulnerable people and so will tend to be attracted to working in schools and hospitals, national broadcasters, youth groups and religious leadership. 'This large organization with a huge amount of public trust ended up harbouring a predator' is a reason for inquiries and new systems, but it's not necessarily an indication of fundamental rottenness.

And there are people – quite a lot of people – who are very willing to pretend that the part is the same as the whole. They are often people who will make a lot of money out of destroying the previous systems. Henry VIII may have sincerely believed that the monasteries were bad through and through. He also did get to take all of their wealth for himself when he destroyed those institutions of societal support: their libraries, chronicles and houses of learning.

At the time of writing, the wealthiest man in the world is Elon Musk. He has shown himself very willing to buy up a media organization, Twitter, and to encourage it to prioritize his viewpoints. He was willing, for example, to encourage rioting in the UK. The venerable American newspaper the *Washington Post*, which has been a byword for investigative reporting even against a sitting president since it broke the Watergate scandal, is now owned by billionaire Jeff Bezos. On 26 February 2025, Bezos posted the following statement about 'a change coming' to the *Washington Post*'s opinion pages:

> We are going to be writing every day in support and defense of two pillars: personal liberties and free markets [...] Viewpoints opposing those pillars will be left to be published by others. There was a time when a newspaper, especially one that was a local monopoly, might have seen it as a service to bring to the reader's doorstep every morning a broad-based opinion section that sought to cover all views. Today, the internet does that job.

I would strongly suggest that the internet does not, in fact, do that job. The internet allows every person, within their little enclosed pew, to access precisely the opinions that most please or enrage them — being enraged is a particular form of being pleased, actually. Finding things on the internet to 'hate read' is a way of feeling great about yourself because you're not as stupid and wrong as those other people. The internet allows and encourages us to either find opinions that we wildly, enthusiastically agree with or conversely the most ridiculous and objectionable and stupid forms of the views on the other side of any issue.

In every information crisis, there is a tendency to cut oneself off and look not at the community around us but at the particular information we want to look at that makes us feel comfortable and right. What we lose via giving in to that tendency is *shared consensus reality*. That is, a reality we all consent to. Once you've lost that, it's easy to dehumanize others, to start to believe that people who disagree with you aren't really people at all.

The job that the *Washington Post* and other broad-based

news outlets used to do was the opposite of the box pews – it would present a range of views but each of them ideally fairly measured, reasonably sensible, at least mostly based in fact. Yes, they failed many times, sometimes catastrophically, to keep to that mission. But that was what they tried to do. The point is: when they showed us views we didn't agree with, they were mostly not finding the *worst* way to present those views but the best.

This is not about a specific viewpoint. If you're reading this thinking, 'Naomi wants me to find x view reasonable and I just don't': no. That's not it. I don't care about the specific viewpoints as much as I care about being able to have civil discourse on contentious issues.

This is about not treating people as symbols. About the sense that we are not surrounded by cretinous vicious imbeciles but mostly by careful thoughtful people who may disagree with us but usually have good reasons for doing so and with whom we could have a reasonably civilized conversation and find many points on which we do agree. I know that saying this already makes me sound like a utopian. I know that it feels right now like we probably *are* surrounded by cretinous vicious imbeciles a lot of the time. That's because we're already right in the middle of an information crisis.

This job of trying to present difficult questions in a fairly reasonable way, the job of basically trying to discover and report the truth, the job that American billionaire-owned media has given up in favour of promoting 'personal liberties and free markets', is the job that the BBC is still doing. It is one of a small and decreasing number of organizations still doing that. If we lose it, we will never get it back and we and the world will be quite a bit closer to the kind of fundamental breakdown of civil discourse that ends up with burning people at the stake.

In Britain we lucked into having the BBC as a result of a paternalistic and other deeply troubling kind of Empire, wealth that we acquired in often dubious ways, a particular class hierarchy. All of that is worth questioning. Every single bit of the BBC's output is worth questioning. This is absolutely not a call for a lack of protest, in fact the opposite. An information organization is alive when it's engaging with the people who use it, when it hears from them, when it's the subject of debate. If you live in the UK, or if you don't live in the UK but you enjoy or rely on the BBC's output, keep on challenging and questioning it. Write angry letters. Write to your MP, to the Prime Minister. Demand the return of *Points of View* with Anne Robinson, or Robert Robinson or presumably someone else with the surname Robinson. Tony, maybe? Colin? Ask for a channel on iPlayer devoted to videos complaining about BBC programmes and answers or reflections on them from BBC producers. Just don't give up on it.

The BBC has a million problems. It deserves challenge again and again. But the basic principle that we need a publicly funded organization to protect the informational health of the country – and to a certain extent the world – is vital. This is what defends us from the rise in utter nonsense. We really won't know what we've got here until it's gone. Try not to let it be gone.

mapping the inner world

I've just turned fifty, an age when I'm finding myself looking both forward and back.

Here's something I think that people only twenty years younger than me would find hard to believe: there were so many things we really never used to talk about, before we could talk about them on the internet. So many experiences were intensely private, unsayable until one could say them anonymously, or to strangers, or at an enormous physical distance but with complete immediacy.

For me, an example is a phenomenon called ASMR – a strange delightful tingle, a shiver down the spine, but in a nice way. I get it from people explaining things carefully and slowly to me ... and from stories. Sometimes when I come up with a particularly good plot for a book, I get a tingling buzzing hum that showers like sparks from the top of my head to the soles of my feet.

I had had the strange tingle all my life, but never mentioned it to anyone. There was no place in conversation for it. It was only in 2012, when the online magazine Vice ran an article titled 'What is ASMR? That Good Tingly Feeling No One Can Explain', that I saw a description in a public place of this experience that I'd had for as long as I could remember. It was a shocking, delightful, startling, strangely exposing feeling. 'Oh, it's *not just me!*'

Something important to note about this immediately is that it's a feeling of *both* individuality – something very personal to me – *and* of community. I'm not the only one. I discover more about myself by seeing others talk about themselves. I'm drawn both outward and inward at the same time. I'll come back to that.

Why hadn't I talked about it before? The feeling wasn't some new development caused by the internet. The internet made it *possible* to talk about it, just like printing made it possible for people to talk about that feeling they had of a personal relationship with God, just like the invention of writing made it possible for people to write down, and then re-experience, ponder, reintegrate, their own internal lives.

How has the internet done that? There are some obvious mechanical explanations. Maybe there was never enough space on newsagents' shelves for a magazine dedicated to ASMR, but now there's always space on the infinite internet. And there's a permanence to internet information. Fifty years ago newspaper articles, radio and TV were here-and-gone. If there was an article about ASMR in the paper one day, and I missed it, that was it. There wasn't really a way for me to find it again.

But I think, reflecting deeply on my own thoughts and feelings, that there's a huge psychological component.

I remember letter-writing – while there are certainly collected correspondences and books of letters that are magnificent and wonderfully written, so much letter-writing was actually fairly pedestrian. Most of the letters I sent as a teenager were like most of the texts we send today: 'What time shall I see you at the station on Thursday?'

The 'Postcards from the Past', collated and published by Tom Jackson, say things like: 'Bought a book for 5p at Victoria, at a sale, of W. H. Smiths.' The phrase 'Having a lovely time, wish you were here' was such a common thing to say in a letter or card from holiday that cards sometimes came pre-printed with the message. There is a romance to letter-writing: I love the pen, the ink, the smooth paper, sealing the words into an envelope. But the actual letters were often just saying the accepted things in the normal way – descriptions of scenes and the day, little anecdotes, funny remarks. Not the deep probing of the self that happens now online.

The internet is so *fast*. You don't need to find the stamps and walk to the postbox. You don't think about how to fit the words on to the page and whether you'll need a new sheet of paper. There is something about the internet's speed that evades the internal censor. I can blurt things out before I've really decided whether I want to. Again, I'm not going to say whether this is a good or a bad thing. It's both, it's neither. It just is. The same speed that means one person can blurt out an insult online has also meant that we can catch hold of the tail of an experience that might otherwise have raced past and express it.

I've noticed that many people older than me think of people younger than me as self-obsessed or weirdly fascinated by their identity, by their strange, sometimes fleeting internal feelings, by the minute experiences that make up a life. I think: 'That's an information crisis for you.' Access to these intense personal experiences is the thing that is brand new with this technology. That is the place of exploration. For people in their twenties now, there is no unmapped world left to explore, nor futuristic space journeys to take. The world that people who grew up with the internet are mapping is the world of inner experience. Once you start to look for it, you see it everywhere. You may well have experienced it yourself. There is a real interest in small personal internal states. I think that's one of the things that accounts for the increase in people noticing that they are neurodivergent. I think it accounts for the modern world's increasing familiarity with particular things that some people's brains don't do, or don't do well. Like aphantasia, the inability to create mental images. Or prosopagnosia, the inability to recognize faces. Or one I have – navigational dyspraxia. I really can't find my way anywhere, it is practically disabling; I once managed to get lost in a town on a small Scottish island which had literally three streets. It was only reading on the internet about someone else talking about their dyspraxia which gave me that shock of recognition and sudden rush of relief. 'Oh, it's not just me.'

But of course it's not only neurodivergent conditions that we're finding this way. It's everything. Interests, enthusiasms, interesting reactions to certain aesthetics, sexuality and gender feelings, places and people and cultures we're drawn to, strange sensory experiences. This mapping is the next stage of the individualist revolution that began when someone was first able to write their own thoughts down, privately.

So, to draw some threads together here: communications technologies draw our attention both inwards to our deepest and most personal experiences and then – because they communicate – outwards to other people who share our experiences. It becomes possible both to understand yourself and name yourself in new ways *and* to find commonality with others that you didn't know was there before. These technologies encourage us to pay attention to the ways we didn't know we were the same as some other people and also therefore the ways in which we didn't previously know we were very different.

We've seen that there is a uniformity and a universalism to writing that encourages thoughts about equality, about the things we have in common and the ways we can make decisions together. The invention of phonetic script contributed to the birth of democracy in ancient Athens and to the other institutions that supported democracy and made it possible: the system of jury trials and the theatre. (Juries in ancient Athens had a minimum of 200 members – really very much like a theatre audience.) These institutions are all in a certain sense the same: there are a few people in the centre, pleading their case, making their argument, presenting themselves for consideration. And there's a trust that by a leap of empathy and understanding, a mass of ordinary people can come together to comprehend and assess complex questions. The intellectual and empathic movement between the actor, the politician, the defendant at the centre of the case – the individual – and the jury, the audience, the electorate . . . that's the movement that we become more and more used to as we work with more communication and information technologies.

What happens is a thinking-together. You get the same thinking-together in a democracy, or on a jury, or in an audience all watching the same play. I move my mind to the individual, I become part of collective thinking. Back and forth. That thinking-together is happening again right now, more intensely and more quickly. I have seen the same thought or the same reply to a debating point ripple out across the internet in a matter of hours, sometimes minutes. It can feel overwhelmingly fast, and that's mesmerizing . . . or terrifying. If you miss the moment when everyone changes their mind about something, you can be the one left high and dry.

We've also seen that with that feeling of equality comes a huge unstoppable wave of disintermediation and disruption of old ways of doing things. I've mentioned the BBC as I do happen to be British, but it's not a unique case. The American journalists PJ Vogt and Ezra Klein have talked about a 'media apocalypse'. Fewer people are actually reading news; newspapers are finding it difficult to pay for war reporters, all journalism has turned into 'clickbait'. News sites are closing, journalism is coming under threat as a profession. Well, we can all see the world through everyone's phones now, can't we?

The same thought flickers through the system incredibly quickly, massively powerfully – turning against ideas and institutions that previously rubbed along adequately for centuries. It's been called 'cancel culture' and it's been labelled a left-wing phenomenon. But I don't think this is a right-wing/left-wing thing. It seems to me that the rapid single-minded change of attitude that makes some left-wingers call for 'problematic' people to be fired is identical to the feelings that led a British newspaper to title an article about anti-Brexit figures 'Crush the Saboteurs' or call them 'enemies of the people'. What are the conspiracy theories about left-wing politicians being Satanists if they're not some kind of 'cancellation'? In these febrile moments it becomes easy to believe that the only way through is to discard anyone who disagrees with us.

Thinking-together can be extraordinarily powerful, a force-multiplier of human intelligence. It can also be insular, damaging and dangerous. No one ever created a system where everyone even *appeared* to agree without having committed a really large amount of atrocities. And every information crisis creates new ways to disagree and therefore new reasons for terrible actions.

Here are the two least emotive examples I can think of. First, there's a highly amusing internet phenomenon, 'Everything is Cake'. A video shows some object – a rubbish bin, a shoe, a television – which is then sliced to show that it's actually cake. It's a joke about a real thing – the more we experience the world through screens, the harder it is to test for ourselves whether what we're seeing is real. It's funny because it's true: the more information there is, the more things we could be wrong about. Even whether or not something is cake.

Second, there was a fun internet storm in 2015 about whether a particular dress was black and blue or white and gold. People got really quite heated about it. I think that underneath that humorous dress debate there was a real and frightening truth. It's becoming clear to us now that apparently reasonable people really do see the same things differently, and you can't always just slice it down the middle to see if it's cake or not. Something that looks obviously one way to you may be obviously another way to someone else. When we talk about the story of the British Empire and colonialism, for example, it's now obvious that a history that looks glitteringly gold and white to one person may seem from another perspective to be beaten black and blue. We look at each other with incomprehension. The silly dress argument was an emotional repetition of a very serious one. How can you *possibly* see it that way when it's obviously this way?

It used to be hard for me to imagine how so many people got so exercised about the abstruse question of whether the bread and the wine *really* becomes the body and blood of Christ, or whether it's just a *symbol* of the body and blood of Christ. Not just exercised, not just pamphlets or speaking strongly – it turned into physical violence, governments toppling, wars fought, people burned at the stake. It's . . . less hard for me to imagine that now.

Just for a moment, imagine having been someone who really believed that your village's beautiful golden cross housed a tiny holy fragment of Jesus's *true* cross. And then comes the Reformation, and someone tells you that if all such relics were real, there'd have been enough wood in the true cross to build a ship. That's a horrifying thought. (It might not actually have been true anyway, but the thought itself is very difficult.) Suddenly everything is up for question. This is one of those psychological changes

I'm talking about. Coming to believe that the special, blessed sliver of holy wood was ... just a splinter would put people in a psychological frame of mind to feel that anything anyone said to them might be a lie.

There is a lot of falsehood out there now. PolitiFact's Israel fact-checking site says that 71 per cent of the claims that it has checked about Israel are false, including false reports of, for example, both a missile strike on Israel and a missile strike *by* Israel. Vladimir Putin is known to run 'troll farms' which encourage anger and argument online. A news analysis by MIT found that 'falsehood dominates online' and that 'false information outperforms true information' with a false story more likely to 'go viral' than a true one.[4] Even the online encyclopedia Wikipedia has to constantly battle editors trying to add in false information: some of them are likely to be state actors trying to bend the truth to benefit their government. It's only getting worse as AI presents itself as a neutral voice while copying false information from online sources. More and more, it's hard to know whether you're even interacting with a real person online or with a bot or a large language model, or a scammer who might themselves actually be held prisoner. These are extremely serious problems. It's usually *possible* to find out whether something is really true or not – the fact-checking organizations I talked about earlier like Snopes and PolitiFact are very useful – but that often involves quite a bit of sometimes very time-consuming online research work.

It's not stupid to be anxious or to feel that truth is under attack. We're learning that truth is extremely complex. It's hard to bear. We don't have the cognitive resources or the tools — yet — to cope with it. So there's always the temptation to insist on our version of the truth alone, that all other versions of the truth are evil and corrupt.

As we've seen, by allowing us to reflect on and share our most intense inner experiences, these technologies draw us both inward and outward. They create new forms of deep commonality with some, and therefore they deepen and solidify our divisions with others. My group is right. Your group is wrong. Not just wrong: evil. And once you believe that . . . well, it gets a lot easier to justify, for example, a bunch of human rights atrocities. And many of the new-technology systems we have now are not helping to make that better; in fact they might be deliberately making it worse.

the idea of a library

Jorge Luis Borges's short story *The Book of Sand*, published in 1975, is about a man who comes into possession of an infinite book. When you hold the book, it is somehow impossible to turn to the first page or the last. However many pages you turn, there are still more between your fingers and the covers. The narrator receives the book from someone who is only too keen to get rid of it, a man who asks for a large sum but doesn't bother to count the money he's paid.

Borges's narrator soon finds out why possession of the book is as much a curse as a blessing. Even though he can't read the words in the book, he cannot stop leafing through it to look at the pictures. Scrolling – as we might say – night and day, he becomes 'a prisoner of the book, I almost never went out any more'. He begins to list the illustrations by writing them in a notebook; they never repeat and his notebook is soon full. He can barely sleep and when he dreams it is only of the book.

In the story, the narrator realizes at last that the book is 'a nightmarish object, an obscene thing that affronted and tainted reality itself'. He does the only thing with it that he can think to do. He takes the Book of Sand to the Argentine National Library, loses himself in the stacks and, carefully not noticing where he is, he leaves the book on a shelf.

I think about the Book of Sand a lot these days. There was a time when the only books that existed were finite books, a book that a person could finish, sit back and reflect on. But now, each of us carries a Book of Sand around with us in our pockets. They are absorbing and entertaining. Goodness knows, when I have been in bad distress or physical pain and really needed distraction, sometimes a scroll through the Book of Sand has been a sanity-saver. I don't find smartphones per se monstrous.

But much of what is difficult about the world of smartphone culture is difficult precisely because of the Book of Sand problem. The content will never repeat. There is always something new to look at. There is sometimes no way to go back and look again and find what you just saw. Even without billionaire tech moguls deliberately creating extremely sticky content and using tricks to keep us scrolling, it is just absorbing to look at something that never ends. And, in an even more extreme way than print culture or written-word culture, smartphone internet culture is persistently engaging, fascinating, alarming, threatening.

Borges's solution was to lose his book in a library. And I think the idea of a library has some of the answers.

Libraries, of course, are under threat. We've seen that during an information crisis it can be very easy to get rid of institutions that were working fairly well beforehand. And it's true that safeguarding those institutions and *not* throwing them away is part of getting through an information crisis as well as we possibly can.

It's also true that during a prolonged information crisis, we increasingly need new institutions to get us through.

The whole institution of 'the media', all of the world of print – newspapers, encyclopedias, dictionaries, 'serious' magazines and silly ones, magazines for special interests and weekly periodicals serving particular communities, reference books and textbooks, guidebooks and phonebooks, the Yellow Pages, the traveller's companion, the phrase book – all of these things and hundreds more had to be invented. So for our current information crisis we will need new institutions too. I think the idea of a library – and particularly a public library – will point us in a good direction.

That's a public library as opposed to private libraries owned by individuals, corporate libraries owned by businesses, church libraries, university libraries, school libraries, private members' club libraries, fee-paying libraries – all of which demand that you belong to a certain organization or have certain traits, or at least are willing to fork over your cash to get in.

Public libraries were – and still are, of course – open to anyone who wants a library ticket. All of the types of printed media I listed above were – and often still are – available at a good public library. The idea of a public library is that you can access good-quality information without having to pay for it at the point of use. It's paid for by all of us, via our taxes, because we all agree that a world in which we all have access to the best information is a world that's better for everyone. We all agree that not having much money shouldn't mean that you can't get good information.

Public libraries have evidently thought extremely hard

about their role in the changing world of information and you can often access good-quality reference materials, even databases like JSTOR or newspaper archives, not just via the physical building of the library but also through the library's own apps.

Through my local library services, I can access a huge number of newspapers both from the UK and around the world, but pleasingly I often have to wait twenty-four hours to read those articles. I think that's really rather magnificent, especially as it relates to the Book of Sand problem.

Neil Postman, in his fantastic prophetic book *Amusing Ourselves to Death*, points out that an information glut can be extremely damaging to us. He says: 'Most of our daily news is inert, consisting of information that gives us something to talk about but cannot lead to any meaningful action.' He makes the brilliant point that the only really *actionable* item in the daily news for most of us, most of the time is ... the weather. We might look at information about the crisis in the Middle East, about rising poverty, inflation, the risk of spreading war in Europe or the climate, but on any given day we're not actually going to be able to *do* anything with that information. They're not actionable on the level of 'taking a jumper because it's going to be cold later'. Postman says that constantly being surrounded by information that we can't act on at that oral-culture human level gives us a sense of 'diminished social and political potency'. If it was true in Postman's day of newspapers and magazines, it's even more true now in the age of always-on news and opinions via a smartphone. Fundamentally, like so much else that happens in an information crisis, the more we access this kind of completely unactionable information, the more we feel afraid, angry and out of control.

For me, the local public library's resources are a pretty good rein on my tendencies to immediately want to look at some piece of information that I can definitely do without seeing right now and which will certainly not be actionable. This is because a public library service has been designed to try to serve the public, and not to hook us into an endless outrage-and-hype cycle. In this way, the public library turns the Book of Sand back into pages you can finish.

Investigating what resources are available through your local library and making sure to use them is one way to keep that institution alive – and I do think we need to keep libraries alive – but more importantly than that, public libraries continue to offer an information service that *isn't trying to sell you something* and force you to stay on their sites for as long as possible.

In fact, I would suggest that we need to extend the principles of the free public library much further.

There are enormous democratizing forces around the internet – we can see many more stories, hear many more voices than we could before. Our Book of Sand isn't mesmerizing because it's monstrous, it's often mesmerizing because it is really enjoyable (in my case) to see people woodturning their own egg cups or to listen to basically as many lectures about ancient Greece as I want. It's mesmerizing because of the amount we can see and hear, because of how new some of that is, because of the voices we haven't heard before.

But there is a digital divide in terms of access to information through the internet. Firstly, there is real digital exclusion. The Good Things Foundation estimates that 10 million people in the UK lack the basic digital skills needed to access the modern world. Smartphones are expensive – even the cheap ones are expensive – and they're increasingly essential to access even basic services like doctor's appointments. Secondly, there are many costs to getting online and accessing information now: some of those costs are clear, as when a website runs ads which cover up half the page. Some of those costs are invisible: as in all the sites and apps that are secretly logging what you do there, selling on information about you or using the data about how long you linger on a particular image to create content that is more 'sticky' to you, so you'll remain there longer and longer, and the big tech company that owns them can talk up their 'user engagement' to drive up their stock price.

Some important services are still free, advertisement-free and pretty good: Wikipedia has its problems and biases but is relatively reliable compared to the churn of AI-generated synopses. Project Gutenberg has the full texts of thousands of out-of-copyright books. Archive.org and its Wayback Machine are vital, especially for fact-checking during this rise in utter nonsense and the active destruction of previous forms of the internet. It's extremely significant that these are now fairly *old* sites, founded when the world wide web was still mostly run by youthful tech-utopian idealists. I'd probably even argue that they now qualify as some of those 'old institutions' which need to be protected from the onslaught of the information crisis and the desire to sweep old things away.

So, back to the public library model. A public library isn't there to give you absolutely everything. It solves the Book of Sand problem by introducing a bit of scarcity and a lack of immediacy. And it's not there to make money. It is there as a public service. It will not try to force you to come back again and again or insist that you take out books you didn't really want or keep track of what you're reading and sell that information about you to the highest bidder.

A lot of these questions right now are framed around 'how to keep children safe from smartphones'. But I think that's to miss the point. Compulsively entertaining and engaging Books of Sand are a problem for children for the same reasons they are a problem for adults. We don't suddenly become magically able to deal with all of the subtle ways that technology companies keep us stuck to our phones when we turn eighteen. Instead of pushing for guardrails on these devices for children, we should be insisting that – like any dangerous or addictive product – smartphones always ship with guardrails, for everyone.

What would a smartphone and smartphone apps be like if they worked like a public library? If it was designed as a utilitarian service rather than a grasping needy desperate little Book of Sand, trying every trick to keep you looking at it as much as possible?

It would have an off-button. Really take a moment to

consider what it means that a lot of modern smartphones can't easily be turned off.

It would arrive with its notifications automatically turned off – apart perhaps from phone calls and text messages, things which people tend to want to see in a timely way from their phones. You'd have to proactively switch every notification on. When its apps updated, if they returned to default mode, their notifications would turn off too.

The apps that you look at would default to only showing you things you have *asked* to be shown. It would be impossible for them to show you things you hadn't asked for, unless you specifically requested it. I mean like a library, which does not randomly insist that in order to get your books, you must also have three books of pornography, a book about how much prettier everyone else is than you and a book about the most upsetting and non-actionable things happening in the world right now.

It would be easy to turn 'infinite scroll' off. Infinite scroll, the feature where most social media apps just keep on showing you new content for ever, the feature where they become a Book of Sand, is actually a very recent invention. I remember using social media when it just showed you everything your friends had posted that day and then stopped. No more socials today. Time to get back to real life. Aza Raskin, the man who invented infinite scroll, feels guilty about it now and believes it's made smartphones more addictive.[5] If we are demanding that people own an addictive product in order to, let's say, pay for parking and access GP services, then we ought at least to be insisting that by law the most addictive parts can be turned off.

Smartphones would have another switch, one which easily turned off almost all of their functionality. I have recently bought a 'Brick' device, which I can touch my phone to in order to turn off most of the software on it, leaving me with just a phone, maps, music and my vocab practice app Anki. It was only after I bought it that I considered how *ridiculous* it is that the phone doesn't make it easy for me to disable a pre-set number of apps using just one button. (If you are a software engineer and find it easy to do this on your phone, please just consider that a compliment to your skills; it should be easy for everyone, not just experts.) The conversation about how much attention these Books of Sand absorb isn't new now, it's been going on for a while. It should be simple to reclaim our attention and obvious that most people want to.

It would be easy and straightforward to switch one's phone number from a smartphone to a dumbphone, for the days when you just don't want to carry the whole world of maddening and exhausting opinions around with you.

A smartphone designed by people who care about your wellbeing wouldn't be asking you to log your mental health with it – don't do that, really really don't do that – or even give little passive-aggressive screen-time notifications. A smartphone designed by people who care about your wellbeing would prompt you to choose apps to disable after a certain point in the evening, would ask to be turned off for a certain number of hours in the day. It would presume that in general your life is better if you are not spending all day looking at it and try to facilitate that.

And social media apps would make it extremely easy *not* to see content that you didn't want to see. It would be simple to 'whitelist' accounts, topics, video channels, types of content. That is to say, if social media apps were designed with public service in mind, it would be straightforward to tell them, for example, 'I only want to see my friends' pictures of their family, their pets, their recipes, their updates about their career' or whatever it is that you want to see, without having to confront their political opinions. We are living through a time when we are going to be winding each other up on political, religious and social opinions a lot. It is all right to want to preserve relationships with family members and friends by only seeing their politics when you *choose* to engage with it.

The ability to whitelist is another provision that's often framed as 'we need to do this for the children' – but actually we *all* need this. There are some online services that allow whitelisting for the children's version but not for the grown-up one. This in itself is *terrible* for adults and for children. It creates a cliff-edge where either you're – let's say – under thirteen and you can only see a few child-focused things on the internet, or suddenly you're thirteen and you get the full firehose of internet horror straight in the face. It means childhood is more denuded of opportunities for entertainment and culture – if everything is accessed via a parent's smartphone then how do children play music for themselves, or browse radio stations? And it means that there are no helpful on-ramps where parents can slowly decide over the years which more adult-oriented content they can tell their child is ready for. 'Protecting the children' is a terrible framing for this. We all need technology that at least allows us the *option* to take care of ourselves.

And apps and services would recognize that the information we store on them *belongs to us* and that we should have the absolute right to move from one service to another extremely easily. Just as we have the right to move easily between different ISA providers or different electricity suppliers. Instead of the current laborious workarounds to try to move your friends list to a new social media platform, the information about everyone we followed or friended on a service should be transferable with the touch of a button. Accounts should be permanently deletable simply and easily, with no lingering data storage.

I am saying these things not because I think that any of the big technology companies will do them, or because I think any country is actually going to design its own SocialPhone (although I'd love it if they did). I'm saying these things because I think we have spent a long time treating this new technology as merely a kind of entertainment and because it's now become inextricably involved in essential parts of our lives. Because no one has yet been able to make an information crisis move backwards and we won't either. Because what we actually need, in order to make these technologies less destructive and more constructive and enjoyable for ourselves, is *new laws*. Many of the points I've listed could – and should – be legislated for.

The Books of Sand are always going to be so engaging that it will be hard to look away from them. That's a problem we've not really acknowledged, much less tried meaningfully to do something about it for ourselves – and indeed for our children. And while Borges saw in 1975 that becoming involved in infinite scroll would be immediately isolating, something we're not really talking enough about is how being that engaged with a Book of Sand is inevitably going to make us much more lonely.

loneliness

Writing, printing and then audio recording, video recording and the internet are technologies that replace real people with objects that can tell us – with much greater accuracy – what those real people themselves said and thought in an enormous range of areas.

Each expansion of this communication and recording technology makes it easier to access huge amounts of expertise. I really cannot overstate how useful that is. I do remember what it was like trying to learn knitting or knots from diagrams, trying to understand via manuals how exactly you were supposed to reorient a mysterious flange on your boiler. No matter how good the diagrams or the technical writing, it was still often basically impossible.

About four years ago I managed to fix a tumble dryer in a holiday cottage by following a YouTube video very closely as the friendly encouraging person on the screen showed me how to put my arm into a secret hole underneath the dryer literally up to the elbow and use a credit card gripped between my fingertips to flip open a hidden compartment and pull out a handful of fluff which the tumble dryer apparently likes to store there for its own personal reasons. I would never have thought to look there. Even as I was doing it, the thought crossed my mind that my arm might potentially get bitten off by some previously hidden tumble-dryer teeth. I would not have been able to do any of that before what I'm calling the 'information crisis' but ought actually to call 'the basic ability to get my clothes dry on holiday'.

Really. I'm about to suggest that all of this comes with some complications and difficulties but it also comes with huge advantages. I think most of us have had some experience of this type with the internet now. No one I know owned that brand of tumble dryer. There was no human for me to call. I can't think of a way I would have done it before the internet; there was no bureau of friendly tumble-dryer experts with knowledge of all models to wander over to or call up for a chat late on a Friday evening. It's easy to love a technology you can rely on to help you get sodden clothes dry on a wet weekend in Wiltshire.

Elizabeth Eisenstein's work suggests to me that the same feeling I have that the internet allows me to learn things I just would not have been able to find out any other way also happened after the print revolution. She writes: 'There is simply no equivalent in scribal culture of the "avalanche" of "how-to" books which poured off the new presses, explaining by "easy steps" just how to master diverse skills, ranging from playing a musical instrument to keeping accounts.' Eisenstein even suggests that it was this avalanche which was at least partly responsible for the decline of the apprentice system. This had once been the only way to be trained in a trade; children were often apprenticed to a master young and spent years working for very little or no money as they were taught this valuable knowledge. It's not hard to imagine why the opportunity to just read a series of books that would teach, let's say, the apothecary's art was a more attractive option than spending years traipsing round after a potentially unkind master, hoping for instruction while doing their donkey-work. Eisenstein says that in this way, printed material 'cut the bonds of subordination which kept pupils and apprentices under the tutelage of a given master'.

It is simply, clearly, good for it to be easier to find out true, useful things. Once it's easier, faster and cheaper to record knowledge, people record more knowledge. Whether that's 'how to play the lute' or 'extend your arm up to the elbow into the dark hollow place beneath your tumble dryer, like this. Trust me, it'll be fine.'

And now, having said all of that, the other side. Writing, printing and the internet encourage us to rely on them and not on the people around us. Because there is much, much more stored in there than any human can tell us. Because it gives us access to a huge array of knowledge that no one we know has. As we've seen earlier, Walter Ong suggested that the development of easy-to-learn phonetic script may decrease respect for the elderly because we don't need their memories of earlier events so desperately. I'm going to suggest that Ong's insight is a specialized version of a general case. Writing, then printing, then the internet make us need the contents of *everyone's* brains less. So it encourages us to respect each other less, talk deeply to each other less, trust each other less.

Nobel Prize-winning animal-behaviour expert Nikolaas Tinbergen studied herring gulls and came up with the theory of the 'supernormal stimulus'. Adult herring gulls have a red spot on their bills which herring gull chicks peck at to get their parents to regurgitate food for them. Tinbergen showed the chicks objects with bigger, brighter, redder dots, even a bright red stick. The chicks pecked at all these supernormal stimuli in preference to their parents. The same behaviours can be observed in other animals. Cuckoos take advantage of it when they lay their eggs in other nests – the parent birds feed the cuckoo chick's gaping mouth over their own offspring's normal-size open beaks. Other birds will sit on a big plaster egg with the precise spots that researchers found appeal most to them in preference to their own eggs.

I am not a biologist, Nobel Prize-winning or otherwise, but hearing about supernormal stimuli made sense of a lot of the modern human-centred world to me. We love creating stuff that presses our own buttons. Not all of it is bad. I would say that musical instruments are supernormal stimuli for the human voice. There may have been someone who argued against the invention of the skin drum or the bone flute, but history does not record them and music seems a pretty unalloyed good to me. Similarly, storytelling feels like some sort of supernormal stimulus for 'just the normal events that make up a life'. If you work a long time with stories you start to get the sense that what you're doing *is* a kind of denial of the fundamental shapeless soggy quality of actual life. Of course storytelling can be used for bad ends. But I wouldn't give up the literature of the world in search of some 'normal-stimulus purity'. Art is a supernormal stimulus.

But then ... refined sugar is a supernormal stimulus for sweet fruits, pornography is a supernormal stimulus for actual sex, videogames can be a supernormal stimulus for many forms of attainment including 'creating order' and 'working towards a goal', and in fact I suspect internet scrolling to be a supernormal stimulus for human enjoyment of learning new things. All of these, genuinely, can be enjoyed in a perfectly lovely way; there are ethical and non-damaging ways to have delight in any of them. We just need to be aware that we might have a tendency to replace *the thing itself* with the very red ball or red stick or the giant plaster egg. It gets bad when sugar has taken over our taste for ordinary mildly sweet fruits, when mesmerizing porn stops us from pursuing consensual enjoyable sex, when we consistently choose videogames over real attainment or scrolling over education.

All of this has been a long way to say: I think writing, printing and the internet might be a supernormal stimulus for 'the companionship of other actual humans'.

I am obviously not arguing that we need to stop reading. I've written a book, you're reading it, the reason that this is a supernormal stimulus is that you get my best ideas here in a concentrated form which you can take in at your leisure without having to say, 'Naomi, you've been lecturing at me for ninety minutes now without pause and, while the things you're saying are quite interesting, I really need a wee and a KitKat. Not at the same time.' Reading is good. It's an accelerator of thinking. *And also* . . .

Here is what the writer Catherine Shannon wrote in a brilliant post on her Substack called 'Do You Remember

How Life Used to Feel?' about her experiences giving up using a smartphone. Just one week after she stopped using her smartphone she observed that: 'People are already a bit more interesting to me. When I had my iPhone with me, I had what felt like the sum of all human knowledge in my pocket, coupled with an instant communication line to all of my friends and acquaintances. Seriously: who can compare? Now, I feel like every person I meet might teach me something. My conversations are literally more interesting, probably because I am allowing myself to be bored.'

This is the box-pew problem again, it's the not-respecting-older-people problem again, it's the Tiv genealogy problem again. It's the problem that arises when our information technologies are so good that they make us turn away from actual people and moment-to-moment experience of life as it happens.

I'm not going to say that everyone has to give up using a smartphone – and Shannon doesn't say that either, although her work is very convincing on the general principle that using them a *lot* less is likely to be better. And 'smartphones' aren't the same as 'the internet'; Shannon still uses the internet from her laptop, she just doesn't – as she says – carry 'the sum of all human knowledge' around all day in her pocket, and it's enabled her to increase the quality of her real human interactions. I have personally done some wonderful thinking-together, including around topics in this book, with people on Bluesky; there is incredible thinking-together happening on many corners of the internet. It's exciting, it's joyful, I am not interested in rolling it back and I think it'd be pointless to try. I think that just like many other supernormal stimuli we've invented, 'internet' is better with some limits. And it's more genuinely enjoyable and useful if it's not replacing the original stimulus: connection with other people in our lives.

In this context I do find it a bit sinister, actually, that AI companies are positioning themselves as offering some kind of imaginary friend. I've used Anthropic's large language model Claude quite successfully to reword difficult-to-understand articles that I've needed to read, to create a to-do list for me from my notes, and I even got it to comment for me on a draft of this book to see what happened when I asked it to give me a critique. It can be a useful piece of technology. (It's never, thus far, produced a sentence I wouldn't be embarrassed to publish as my own work, and this isn't even to get into the IP theft involved in creating these models and siphoning their value to a few tech oligarchs. If we urgently need a smartphone that works like a public library, the need for a large language model that works like that and is funded and distributes its income like that is even more desperate.)

But a breathless article in the *New York Times* calling Claude 'San Francisco's most eligible bachelor' and saying that its 'killer feature' is 'emotional intelligence', as if it could take the place of a boyfriend, set all my supernormal-stimulus alarm bells ringing.

The article says that Claude's so-called emotional intelligence 'isn't something that can easily be measured' but, er, as a novelist I found it rather easy to tell what Claude is doing. It starts every piece of writing with a compliment and ends with a follow-on question encouraging more conversation. When I asked it to comment on the last few paragraphs it started with 'I think the draft looks really thoughtful and engaging!' because of course it did. This is the stuff that real humans do often forget to do when giving feedback. And it was nice to get that feedback immediately I finished writing at 9 p.m. on a Sunday night, rather than waiting for my editor to get back from holiday. Claude never tires of paying compliments and delivering occasionally helpful critique. It pushes our human buttons so hard to have something to talk to that is always available, always friendly and positive, always wants you to talk more. And how different this is from a genuine conversation with an actual person, with all its potential for being frustrating and unsatisfying.

There is money to be made out of supernormal stimuli, which hasn't gone unnoticed. Mark Zuckerberg gave an interview on 30 April 2025 about the future of AI, commenting that 'the average American has fewer than three friends [. . .] and the average person has demand for [. . .] fifteen friends'. His suggestion – well, let's be honest, his business plan – is that 'as the personalization loop kicks in, as the AI gets to know you better and better [. . .] that will be really compelling'.

The thing is that, like any other supernormal stimulus, if we overuse them these technologies do leave us starving for more of what they lied they were going to provide. AI may have some transformational uses, but if we rely on it for human connection over real people, it will leave us more lonely. Loneliness is a profound problem in wealthy countries which have become highly individualist. Many studies have been written on what's now called 'the loneliness epidemic'. There are a lot of reasons for it – as ever, just because I'm focusing on technology in this book, that doesn't mean that technology is the only thing we need to think about. People in wealthy individualist countries tend to live further from their extended family and friends, and tend to participate in organized religious life less; these are two major ways that people have found for sustaining community and many wealthier countries have just thrown them out without replacing them with any other mechanisms for creating community and combating loneliness.

Certainly it's also true that the pandemic increased loneliness hugely; not being able to see each other in person is definitionally something that makes people more lonely. I'd also argue that our current technologies have enabled us to keep on doing our pandemic behaviours even now that most people have been able to have all the vaccines we want and don't need to do social distancing any more. Is that a bad thing? Not for immune-suppressed people and people with other disabilities and access needs who were arguing for years that – for example – live events ought to be streamed online so that people who couldn't be physically present could still enjoy that education or entertainment. It must have been quite infuriating for campaigners who'd been told for years that this type of access was too hard, but then suddenly once there was a global pandemic it was easy.

But with these technologies, it's pretty much always both a good thing and a bad thing. To take an example from my own life: I love the Open University in the UK and I've been studying various things with them for more than a decade now. Before the pandemic we used to have the opportunity to meet up in person about once every couple of months at tutorial events. It was a real highlight, getting to chat to the other students and with flexible time to ask the tutor any questions. It felt very special to make time over a weekend for this personal interest that's important to each student in different ways, to head out for a coffee together after the tutorial, to moan about things together or share inspiration. It felt like a community. Those in-person tutorial events went away during the pandemic and never came back. Instead we get a boundaried brief one-hour scheduled online tutorial where there's no opportunity for conversation, to see each other's faces or discuss our difficulties.

This is just one example of the way that technology – while allowing brilliant access for some people – can diminish the personal human warmth and flexibility that create a supportive community. Learning is still happening very well via the Open University. But not so much, perhaps, the connections that diminish loneliness.

Coming at the loneliness question from a different direction, there's a common phrase used in social justice circles: 'It's not my job to educate you.' I understand where this comes from. Sometimes, as a fat person, as a Jewish person, as a queer person, as a woman – or simply as a person who exists on the internet – I get questions from strangers that are exhausting; I've answered them so many times before, it is easy enough for the person asking to just *do an internet search* and find the answer. I have been known to reply to questions from strangers online by typing the question into an internet search box and sending that link to the questioner. (To be honest, I mostly do that about tech-support questions.)

But I'm making my own point for myself here. Sometimes people are asking bad-faith questions in a bad way just to get a rise out of me, for sure. But sometimes asking a question is a part of a relationship. When I was an undergraduate, I was the first Orthodox Jewish person most of the people in my college had ever met. For quite a number of them, I was the first Jewish person they'd ever met. I had to answer the same questions over and over about kosher food, about the Sabbath. There was no Google in 1993, there was no way for them to 'educate' themselves. Even if they'd gone to the library to find a religious studies textbook, my experience of most of those textbooks was that they were wrong. Those questions began conversations which were how we formed relationships. It was pretty easy to tell from a brief conversation whether the person I was talking to was genuinely interested in learning about what I was doing and why, and pretty easy also to tell who was just an arsehole.

What's happened now is that it's very easy to internet-search 'what is kosher food' and receive a fairly accurate answer. So a technology exists which can replace a certain amount of conversation. Which, in aggregate, leads to fewer boring annoying hostile aggressive upsetting conversations – probably good! – but also fewer conversations in general and especially about hard topics . . . maybe not so good. Particularly when we consider that relationships form through rupture and repair, by struggling through hard and awkward conversation and learning about each other in the process.

Fundamentally, the only way you discover whether you can trust other people is by trusting them a bit and seeing what happens. If they have the opportunity to harm you and don't, that's one good piece of evidence that they're trustworthy. The way that communities form is by having to rely on one another. Everyone being tremendously independent and being able to do everything alone . . . leads to loneliness.

As I hope will be clear by now, none of this is an argument to get rid of these technologies. It's *great* to be able to sit at home and learn a range of new skills or find out things you never knew before about where a strange tumble dryer stores its fluff. It's really respectful towards someone from a different culture to go and have a little read online so that you can approach what they're doing with extra knowledge and be able to ask insightful questions. In the same way it was great after the advent of printing for people who wanted to learn music or recipes to be able to read a book rather than spend their life seeking out someone to teach them. And it's great that when we want to know what happened eighty years ago we don't always have to find a ninety-five-year-old person and ask them.

It also leads to less social connection and more loneliness. It can get compulsive in a supernormal-stimulus way, encouraging us to prefer online scrolling to real human interactions. Which leads to even more loneliness. It can mean we get more frightened of the hard conversations that enable us to create strong meaningful friendships. Which creates, yes, yet more loneliness.

If you're feeling more isolated than you were just a few years ago, this might be the reason. Like every problem I've identified in this book, the solution isn't 'banning', and it's not just 'personal responsibility' either. A Book of Sand that works more like a library would help. New social norms will help. New behaviours will help. I have some suggestions near the end of the book. But fundamentally: start by understanding that loneliness isn't just something that's happening to you because you've done something wrong. It's an artefact of the historical era we're living through. Make an arrangement to see someone, in person. Your friends would like to hear from you.

a fast machine

In the novel *Orlando* by Virginia Woolf, a gender-changing protagonist lives without ageing for centuries, and so experiences the way that the pace of life has sped up. Late in the novel, Woolf describes driving in a car through modern London like this:

> Here was a market. Here a funeral. Here a procession with banners upon which was written 'Ra--Un' [. . .] Nothing could be seen whole or read from start to finish [. . .] After twenty minutes the body and mind were like scraps of torn paper tumbling from a sack and, indeed, the process of motoring fast out of London [. . .] resembles the chopping up small of identity.

This is how new technologies work. Things get faster and faster. Printing a book is faster than copying it by hand. Posting on social media is faster than sending a letter. That's basically the purpose of technology. It lets us do things we could do before, but easier and faster. Or it lets us do new things, which means that the pace of change feels faster.

Eventually, we get used to the speed. We find ways to manage it. The speed of a car doesn't startle us any more. It's when the technology is new, before we've learned to manage it, that we most experience that fragmentation.

My suggestion is that that's when social norms tend to be most open to change too. It's frightening, and it's also exciting. *Orlando* was published in 1928, the same year that women in England, Wales and Scotland got a right to vote that was equal with men. Orlando's change from 'him' to 'her' as Orlando sped through the centuries was a true representation of rapid social change after the First World War. Men and women were more alike than they'd ever been. The torn scraps of paper rearranged themselves into a new social order.

The philosopher Peter Singer has written about an 'expanding circle' of who is considered truly part of our in-group over the past centuries. Others have further enlarged that idea to talk about the 'expanding circle of us'. This is the thought that as humans we have grown able to see people who are increasingly different from us as still 'like us', still deserving the rights, freedoms and privileges of humans. No change is universal, of course. But broadly, over the millennia, the idea of a fundamental human equality has spread. At one time, only kings had what you might call a 'vote' – they decided what happened. Slowly, the idea spread that maybe all the *nobles* could participate in making decisions. Then, maybe it was all men who owned property. But probably they were white, able-bodied Christian men. We've thought wider and wider. Maybe, we've thought, all humans are people, no matter our skin colour, ethnic roots or religion? Maybe people with disabilities are still people, maybe LGBT+ people are people, maybe *women* are people.

This is a simple version of a complex story. Like I say, it hasn't happened everywhere. Or evenly. We don't have a complete record. There's evidence that some ancient and indigenous cultures may have been very egalitarian – the book *The Dawn of Everything* by David Graeber and David Wengrow is very informative on this. The same things don't happen in the same order or line up in the same way. Ancient Athenians absolutely thought that men who have sex with men are people. But they owned slaves and didn't think that women were really people at all. There are always some who call for movement backward. Still, on the broadest level, this is what has happened. And I think what I've been exploring in this book – the revolutions around a series of information crises – is *how* it's happened. Reading and writing, spreading words and ideas faster and faster, it becomes increasingly obvious that there's not a kind of person who isn't really a person. I can't call that anything but wonderful.

I do think we're heading somewhere astonishing with all this. And somewhere that's going to feel frightening and strange to a lot of us.

Imagine what the heroes of the *Iliad* – the men in their glittering armour and flashing swords – would have made of the Abrahamic faiths with their emphasis not on winning honour in glorious battle but on . . . treating other people kindly and trying to love your neighbour as yourself? Obviously those ideals often weren't honoured – in the Crusades, let's say, or indeed the wars of Reformation.

The important thing is that the ideal itself had changed, the idea of what made a person good and worthy had changed. Imagine what Henry VIII would have made of the modern monarchy and of the relationship between Charles III and his kingdom? I think Agamemnon and Achilles, Henry VIII and Mary I (quite a fan of burning-at-the-stake) would all have been horrified by some of the ways we live now. Dispersal of power, growth of strange new ideals about tolerance, acceptance of difference, *not* just letting those in charge kill the people who disagree with them?

Hard as it is to imagine, if we follow the logic of this through . . . the people who come after this current information crisis might also look bizarre to us, and we might look upsettingly inhumane to them.

I can't know what's coming. But if forced to *guess* what could happen that would feel as enormous as that to us . . . I might guess that it's going to become harder and harder to justify the vast inequalities between countries. It's hard already, but somehow we do tolerate it. The faster and better instant translation works, the more we're able to see the lives of people in other countries, the more obvious it will be that in fact people in one country are *no better* than they are in another. So why does one country have so much more wealth?

In 2023, research for the Booker Prize Foundation found that readers under thirty-five are now buying more than six times as many books in translation as retired people. I find that exciting. People who grew up with this information crisis are naturally seeing themselves as more 'the same' as people who live in other countries and speak other languages.

I suspect that the increase in anti-immigrant rhetoric in many of the world's richest countries is – in part at least – a hazy recognition of this inevitable change.

Barring absolute catastrophe – which we can never entirely rule out – the huge increase in new ideas isn't going away. We're going to need to find ways to accommodate them. This has always been the direction of travel of information crises. Even after the previous massive absolute catastrophes, like the collapse of the Roman Empire or the Black Death, the plurality of ideas in books didn't vanish. That's the thing about information revolutions: they create forms of information that can outlast the specific people or even the specific cultures that created them. I don't think there's a way to turn this one back, just like the previous ones were irreversible.

We've seen that there can be a push in an information crisis to make everyone agree with you – it's related to the desire for 'purity' that was part of the Axial Age, to religious wars, wars of interpretation, using force to create agreement. It never works. Eventually, societies learn to enlarge themselves so that people with different beliefs can live together relatively peacefully. I don't think Elizabeth I would have been as horrified by the modern world, perhaps, as her father and sister. She said herself that she didn't believe in making 'windows into men's souls' – some part of the Enlightenment surely starts there. The same forces that caused the Reformation also pushed towards the Enlightenment: the development of print allowed the creation of a 'republic of letters' where people all across Europe forged connections outside their nations and states and started to 'do their own research' and share their findings. The Enlightenment isn't above critique. But we certainly did learn a lot through it.

To get there from here, we can predict that two things are going to happen: there'll be more conflict and there will also eventually be new ways to manage the information we already have.

I'm sorry about the conflict. I wish I could say otherwise but I think it's going to get worse before it gets better – at least that's what history predicts. I've written this in the hope that understanding what we're going through can be some kind of inoculation. If you agree with what I've said, if you also think that at least some of the reason that conversation and debate feel so fraught right now is because of our new communication technologies . . . maybe that helps with taking a step back, not immediately shouting angrily at someone who disagrees with you, online or in real life. Having thought about this a lot: increasingly I take everyone's emotions seriously . . . and very few people's opinions. Everyone's got an opinion. Unless the person is an expert it's a mistake to treat their opinion as very important.

We're going to be living through a mechanical change in technology for the rest of our lives which will – for the rest of our lives – make us more psychologically prone to feeling that extreme punishments are justified for people who aren't 'on our side'.

I think it's worth remembering that in general, these

days, we don't look back with horror on the European Reformation's wars of religion because people believed in transubstantiation or because they didn't. We look back in horror because of the things they ended up doing when justified by righteousness in either of those beliefs. In England, Catholic monarchs executed Protestants and Protestant monarchs executed Catholics. If someone else can now detect a difference in mercy or kindness between either side, I really can't.

all right, but what am I supposed to do about all this?

Some of this isn't solvable on an individual level. As I've already mentioned, as a generation – as several generations – of people going through a prolonged information crisis, we need good new laws that recognize the protective institutions we already have and shore them up, while also preventing what are now massively wealthy technology companies from using their power to stir up more dissent and distress in this already very volatile time.

So: the first thing we can do is to write to our representatives and say: 'This is important to me, please address it.'

We're also going to need new ideas to get us through, and I don't have them all. We're going to need to develop whatever is the equivalent of a curriculum, a textbook, an indexed resource which condenses millions of people's ideas into a single step-by-step outline, and by which we can teach ourselves and our children how to manage this new firehose of information and opinion. We might need to rethink the whole concept of childhood again. We'll have to invent robust and flexible new systems to teach ourselves and our children 'the good stuff' out of the flood of information, and teach the skills of finding new 'good stuff'.

If you're reading this and feeling that I might be right about what's happening, and you want to do something useful with your life: either get involved in solutions to climate change and habitat destruction, or see if you can come up with whatever is the internet version of a textbook and a curriculum. I don't know what those things are but we desperately need them. I don't rule out the idea that some kind of large language model might help with synthesizing the amounts of information around. But a large language model would only be able to do that if it's been trained on information that is *true* and probably if it is *not* owned by the kind of technology billionaires who have proven themselves to be bad stewards of our collective value and values. And I rather suspect that in the future that kind of truth is going to be charged out at a high cost. Which won't help the majority of people. If you want to make something that might really help, here are some questions to ask:

- How can I find out the *real facts* underlying some of these very difficult culture-war questions? Even if the 'real facts' are 'no one is absolutely sure, and if they say they're sure, they're lying'? What does it mean now to be Tycho Brahe, doing very accurate observations? How can we make the most accurate observations accessible and easy to understand for the largest number of people?
- How can I make systems of communication that *best mirror* the things we do naturally in person – noticing when someone is upset, talking about many things not just one thing, remembering the wholeness and humanity of the person I'm talking to?

- How could we work on and propagate good new social and cultural norms about the way we use the internet? 'Just ban it' isn't going to work, nor 'just ban it for x group'. Especially if that group is teenagers, who have a tendency to get around bans. What are the most important and wonderful things we do on the internet and how can we encourage more of those and less of the hateful stuff?
- What are the laws and governmental systems that will make our information systems work for all of the people, not just a few billionaires? How can new technologies be harnessed to enable law and regulation to keep pace with the change, rather than constantly running ten to twenty years or more behind it?
- How can we make the new version of the public library or the textbook that guides me through what I need to know online? What are the simplifying forces which will help me feel that I am accessing the information I need without becoming overwhelmed?
- What does education need to be now? How can we guide children towards what is best in internet use, towards creating meaningful relationships and friendships, towards that fundamental equality that these technologies encourage, without getting sucked into the compulsive qualities of the supernormal stimulus? How do we do that for ourselves?

There may well be another Enlightenment on the far side of all this – I think there probably is. We need to get there as fast as possible. If you have some ideas, please get working on it.

Now, if you're reading this and you're satisfied with your job and not immediately in the market for a radical change of life-purpose, how to get through the information crisis on an individual level? In the Reformation there were people who got very into burning-at-the-stake and there were people who quietly got on with their lives as best they could, trying not to fall out with their neighbours too much, and we all know which we'd rather discover our ancestors were.

Incidentally, here's a thing to consider: unless the world totally collapses, which can never be *entirely* ruled out, future generations will probably be able to find out rather a lot about us. Exponentially more than could be discovered about people who died without ever being on social media. Related to the question about rights to forget and be forgotten: one of the effects of these new technologies is that many, many more people have a *legacy* after each new technology is invented. In the same way that, like the ancient Sumerian kings, we can now insult any king we like, we are the first generation in history to all have what would previously have been a monarch-level of legacy – through everything from the memes we repost, the photographs and videos we take, the comments we leave on other people's work. As they say in *Hamilton*, history really does have its eyes on us. We won't be here to see what they make of us in the future, but they'll be making something of what we've written and recorded.

There probably are things we can do on an individual level which will make us less cringeworthy forebears. Or more importantly, people who we don't have to regret being.

To start with, I think it helps just to understand that, for all the reasons we've been looking at in the previous chapters, we all have a greater impulse during this information crisis towards a kind of fundamentalism. And having understood this, to try to resist it even though it feels uncomfortable, annoying, boring and maybe even *wrong* not to act on first impulses.

I'm not saying that you're wrong in your view on whatever topic it might be, or that it's not an important subject. I'm saying that the reason it feels *so* heated and overwhelming and impossible to look away from is the information crisis.

So. Don't let the worst 'the other side' has done become the new low bar for your own behaviour. Don't treat people as symbols. Consider the possibility that where reasonable people disagree there may be some useful truth on both sides, even if it's only the truth of – as we say these days – 'lived experience'. Don't try to get anyone fired today. Don't insult or berate someone today. Don't trawl through someone's social media going back decades to dredge up the worst thing they've ever said, today. Don't, fundamentally, burn anyone at the stake today.

I have a good friend who disagrees with me on a hot-button culture-war topic. It doesn't really matter which one, although you're welcome to amuse yourself guessing. Just think of a culture-war-style subject on which you've disagreed with a friend and felt upset. And let's call my friend Lorna, because that's not her name.

Lorna and I have been through about eight years now of talking and arguing about this hard topic. It has sometimes been very heated and we've both got quite distressed at points.

I believe that she holds her view sincerely and she believes the same about me; so at least we've avoided one of the easiest traps to fall into, that of accusing the other person of not thinking what they say they think, of just 'virtue-signalling' or some other words for 'I just don't believe you'. If giving advice I'd probably start there: don't tell a Catholic or a Protestant that they don't really believe what they say they believe about transubstantiation. Accusations of 'You don't really think that, you're just saying it to get attention', or whatever, will get you nowhere good. Just a few steps closer to the flaming pyre.

I have seen other people have deep and important friendships torn apart over this topic. I think it's important – if you can – not to let that happen to your friendships. The information crisis will already drive us to rely on media rather than on each other, to become increasingly lonely, isolated, depressed and paranoid. It will drive us to believe more and more extreme things, and to begin to believe that 'the other side' to us on any argument isn't really quite human at all. Trying to preserve friendships across culture-war topics is a way we avoid doing those destructive, cruel things that demean and erode us as human beings.

It doesn't have to mean agreeing. It means not allowing disagreement to become a reason to end a relationship.

I don't say that anyone *has to* maintain a relationship. You must judge for yourself whether your own relationships are worth preserving. I don't know your friends or family and it's for you to decide if a relationship is damaging for you and whether you need to step away. But if both of you are fundamentally decent people who just happen to disagree, if neither of you has in fact burned anyone at the stake yet, it's probably worth trying.

Not having yet burned anyone at the stake – or other related behaviours – is quite a good test too. I said to Lorna quite early on in these conversations that if she became someone who harassed people online who she disagreed with, that would be a red line for me. There's a difference between disagreeing with a dear friend in private conversation and turning into someone who shouts at strangers about it, or worse. Lorna pointed out very reasonably that she'd never harassed anyone about anything. Which was a good lesson for me too: I had already started to think of people who were more aligned with her viewpoint as 'those people', the kind who harass others online.

This is an important point. If you don't manage to maintain friendships 'across the line' of any cultural divide, you will end up only hearing from the most extreme people on the other side of the line. Because those are the people who are willing to shout about their views in public – and the more extreme they are the more frequently they're shouting about them. So your view of people who disagree with you – my view of them – would have got worse and worse.

Lorna and I have, I think, gained a great deal from being able to remain friends. The world feels less frightening, violently angry and disgraceful to us. Because we can check in with each other and say, 'I heard someone "on your side" say this hateful thing, do you agree with that?' and, basically, we never do agree with the hateful stuff. We're just here, holding our views, not thinking insane, distressing or revolting thoughts. It makes the information crisis less of an existential 'I never really knew half my friends' crisis.

What have Lorna and I done that's worked? Neither of us are experts on this particular topic, we don't have degrees in related fields, we don't work in it. I think it helps that we can both recognize that what we come up with is 'reckons'. This is what I reckon. We're not forming public policy in that area, and we're both able to say the critical words 'I might be wrong about this.' The most we're doing is saying: 'This is what I reckon.'

I think it also helps that I have in my life already figured out how to be friends across a religious or quasi-religious divide. I grew up an Orthodox Jew. I'm not an Orthodox Jew any more, not because I hate it or think it's a bad way to live – it's actually in many ways a very good way to live: community-focused, interested in education and in raising children with strong values of charity, tolerance, generosity. Orthodox Judaism tells its members to do *mitzvot* – an untranslatable word somewhere between a good deed and a commandment – like visiting the sick, caring for the elderly, spending time with mourners; even teaching your children to swim is a *mitzvah*. Orthodox Jews observe a weekly Sabbath with no screens allowed – given everything I've written about in this book, this feels like a genuinely excellent idea! – and there are strict rules around kosher food, and other things. I don't hate it, I have my disagreements with some parts of it which I've written about elsewhere, and the life of strict rules isn't for me. I stopped being an Orthodox Jew in my early thirties but I never stopped respecting many of its ideas and I've managed to maintain very dear friendships and strong relationships with my Orthodox Jewish family.

Lorna and I talked early on about what happens between me and my Orthodox friends – in a system where things are clearly 'working'. The answer is, to some extent, I don't talk about religious observance with my Orthodox friends and family. There's no need, there are plenty of other things to talk about, they have understood what I do and don't do. When I'm in their homes I'm respectful of their way of living. When they visit me, I would never feed my friends or their children food that didn't meet their kosher-food standards. We *could* sit and have endless arguments about our small areas of disagreement but what would be the point? What, actually, is the point supposed to be of these endless culture-war arguments, other than keeping us glued to our screens and devices?

Religious communities have been working out how to live relatively peacefully together for hundreds of years – since the last information crisis, in fact – and they have a lot of wisdom for us about how to do it. I'm far from the first person to leave Orthodox Judaism but retain close ties with friends and family. The system there is built to make space for that possibility. From a friend who works in interfaith dialogues I've learned that one of the key elements is: *start with what you agree on*. Don't start in on the very hardest questions; don't start with: 'Is this really the body and blood of Christ or just a symbol of the body and blood of Christ?' Start with anything where you can build connection and find shared values. If the debate is fierce, that's almost certainly because there *are* things you really agree on, and it feels particularly shocking to disagree on this one subject.

So Lorna and I have done that – kept talking, sometimes haltingly, sometimes having to really force ourselves to do it, about the things we do agree on. And we've been careful to allow each other to tap out of the conversation. To say: 'Actually I really can't talk about this now.' These days, we ask permission. 'I want to talk about the hard topic, how is that for you?' Sometimes the answer is 'Not today', and respecting that is how everyone feels safe, how conversations don't become overheated, frightening and final.

Something else we've done is to try to have most of our hard conversations in person, or at least over the phone. As I've written about in this book, writing technologies are *incredibly useful* but also each new development abstracts us more from Walter Ong's 'primary orality', the warm, flexible, human-scale world of talk where we can see each other's distress, respond to it, feel empathy with one another. It does not feel a coincidence to me that so many culture wars erupted into uncontrollable anger during the pandemic, when people could not speak to each other face to face.

I asked Lorna what she thinks has gone right for us and she specifically said: 'My decision to leave social media at the start of the pandemic helped me stay relatively sane on the topic. Or at least regain my sanity.' I think the same about having had a locked account on Twitter for all of the years I was on that platform. This stopped me from getting into bad arguments with strangers and saying things in public that I might then have felt I had to stand by in order to be consistent with my former self. I didn't experience random strangers coming to have an argument with me about something I'd said eight years before, which leads to a feeling of defensiveness and then lashing out. These days on Bluesky, which upsettingly has no 'locked account' mode, I have the words 'not getting into pointless arguments on the internet is an act of revolution' in my profile. It keeps me honest. Sometimes I feel tempted to get into a pointless argument. Sometimes someone else has to say, 'I thought you didn't believe in doing this.' And I stand back and go, 'Oh yes, arse, I haven't lived according to my own values here.'

Actually, for all I've said about not wanting an Orthodox Jewish rules-based life, here's a rule I have developed for myself:

> *Never talk about a culture-war topic with anyone who **only** wants to talk to you about that topic.*

Believe me, this will stand you in good stead. These conversations can only be helpful if they happen as part of a relationship. If you're going in cold on a very hard topic, you will not be able to experience each other as people, only as opinions or symbols.

Another piece of actual advice. If you encounter a stranger online who seems basically fine but is sounding really aggro with you, try saying something like this: 'You're sounding quite aggressive, is that what you intended?' This works even better if you do it in a private message. Not everything has to be played out in public, just as we would (hopefully) wait to have things out in private with a friend or partner and not shout at them at a dinner party. *Who's Afraid of Virginia Woolf?* is not a manual for good living.

I can in general strongly recommend *ceasing to expect everyone around you to agree with you.* In this sense, what I'm recommending is a bit of a dose of the Jewish idea that action is more important than beliefs. Or maybe it's simply the idea Elizabeth I got to after seeing her actual family destroy each other – not to mention put the country through years of bloodshed – in the English Reformation. No windows into men's souls. The thing is that in these culture wars it's likely that neither viewpoint will actually be eradicated. And we can't, and don't, demand that people all believe the things we think are correct. There is no 'thoughtcrime'. People can believe whatever they like, inside their own heads, as long as they treat others well.

I know that can feel hard. Our view seems so obvious. Why can't they see it? The dress is white/gold/blue/black.

It's unbearable that they might be thinking that stupid offensive thought in their mind. If we're nice to each other despite these differences, aren't we just pretending? Mustn't we just be honest with each other all the time?

Here is a thought. If someone disagrees with you and still wants to speak to you respectfully and treat you well, perhaps consider that the name for that is love.

Lorna says that the most important thing for her is: 'I feel we have and have always had a shared understanding of what constitutes decent behaviour. It's when you can't accept that your friend believes fundamentally different things from you that the trouble starts. Because there's always going to be that one, really important topic where they do.'

The longer this information crisis goes on, the fewer friends I have with whom I agree on everything, or even most things. Managing that disagreement, agreeing to treat people well even when we disagree with them, is how we stop ourselves from becoming lonely, isolated and afraid.

a wonderful catastrophe

I take the long view, and in the long view I feel fairly hopeful. We are trying to do something quite remarkable as a species, which is to think together. To come to a moral consensus together. To take these brains that evolved to live among smallish groups, a few thousand at most, and find ways to get them to deal with billions. In the past, this has led to the development of moving and beautiful moral sensitivity.

We've done something extraordinary since 2020, something that I think is unprecedented in the history of the planet. We, as a global species spread across the Earth, managed to act together to mitigate a species-wide threat. Fine, not everyone agreed on the right approach to the pandemic. Fine, not everyone did what their governments mandated. In some cases even the members of the government didn't. But across the world scientists shared information across borders and enough of us did some very tough things that the pandemic didn't spread as quickly as it otherwise might have. And we did it – to a large degree – because we could see what everyone else was doing, live through our interconnected screens. We could access news and policy documents from Korea or from Italy, we could watch frightening or uplifting video testimony from China or Germany. We debated whether the Swedish policy was better than the Japanese one. Now we're still discussing whether the approaches we took were the right ones – and when we do that we're not thinking about our neighbourhood or city; we're looking as a species, across the planet.

It's that debate, that thinking-together, that is new. I find it incredibly exciting. It's happened now. It's not going back.

Walter Ong, the great historian of orality and literacy, wrote that the potential of writing is a wonderfully paradoxical thing. Writing 'has the power to liberate us more and more from the [. . .] bias and confusion it creates' itself. We will write ourselves into all sorts of trouble – real moral, spiritual, physical, psychological, intellectual trouble – but we can also use these technologies to work ourselves out of them again.

We made a wonderful, catastrophic thing with writing. With printing. With the internet. It's a kind of raising of the dead. A kind of telepathy. A kind of heaven, where we see each other as thoughts and character, not bodies, wealth or birth. We are making our minds do something they never evolved to do. It's hard, and painful, and often makes us angry and afraid. And yet . . . every time we end by seeing each other more clearly, understanding more, working together. Here we go again.

an afterword: the thing I haven't talked about

This is a book about how information crises affect the humans going through them and have done repeatedly, even when the information crisis happens very organically, driven by people just noticing for themselves that writing a simple-to-learn script is obviously extremely useful or that, my goodness, printed books are so cheap that now we can all own as many as five or even seven of them.

The thing I haven't talked about very much in this book is the way that our current information crisis is shaped by enormous business interests, by money that is being put into exacerbating some of the normal information-crisis problems for profit, and by bad actors who have also worked out what happens during information crises and are using that knowledge to deliberately try to create chaos. That's not because I don't think it's a big part of what's happening.

There are a lot of people already writing and thinking about the part of our current information crisis that is really intentional – or at least is caused by a negligently low level of interest in how to manage an information crisis well.

I would encourage readers of this book to seek out Gabriel Gatehouse's podcast *The Coming Storm*, which is about how certain interests in the United States in particular have deliberately inflamed some parts of the information crisis to get what they want. Also to read Jaron Lanier's book *Ten Arguments for Deleting Your Social Media Accounts Right Now*, and to listen to Timnit Gebru's interview on the podcast *Tech Won't Save Us* entitled 'Don't Fall for the AI Hype'. Books by or informed by whistleblowers inside technology companies are also essential reading: Sarah Wynn-Williams's *Careless People* and Kate Conger and Ryan Mac's *Character Limit* reveal very clearly the people who are running our current information crisis and what their values are. Which is mostly 'increase shareholder value, do anything to exploit our users to make that happen'.

By some quick internet searching I did the following calculation:

In 2024 Facebook generated $164 billion in revenue out of roughly 3 billion users. In the US – one of its most valuable markets – each user was worth about $49.63 to Facebook. US Facebook users spend an average of half an hour a day on the platform. So, about 180 hours a year.

Think about what an hour of your time is worth to you. Think of what a single hour can mean – doing an hour of work and being paid your wage for it, getting some good exercise, reading a book, tidying up the kitchen, an enriching conversation with a friend, time in nature, listening to a great album, having a nap or just staring blankly into space. Think of the value of that.

An hour of your time on Facebook is worth about 24.6 cents to Mark Zuckerberg. That's about 20p. Is an hour of your time worth just 20p to you?

Use social media for what it's useful for, for you. But don't kid yourself that it's not a massive project in the destruction of value so that a few drops of that value end up in the pockets of multi-billionaires. An enormous river of human attention, interest and thinking diverted to disperse away to nothing, so that a little run-off keeps some tech companies' stock value high.

You may feel that this financial part is really the largest piece of the puzzle of the information crisis. I wrote this book partly because I wanted to argue that, no, actually, even without strong financial incentives to keep us staring at our screens, the nature of an information crisis is that a lot of what's happening now just . . . happens. It's happened before, in predictable ways. We can learn from the past about what to expect and how to protect ourselves.

But I think it's obvious that the current technology landscape that our information crisis is taking place in is exacerbating the problems and making it harder to find solutions. This is the reason that a lot of what we need are strong laws and confident governments who know that a massively important part of their job now is providing us with as many bulwarks as possible against the worst parts of the information crisis.

The other thing I haven't talked about much in this book is AI. There are plenty of great writers trying to work out what the development of large language models (LLM) and other kinds of generative AI will mean for the world. I'm thinking a lot about it myself – I can recommend a podcast episode from the *Financial Times Economics Show* where Martin Wolf, the chief economist of the *FT*, talks to David Autor about what kind of threat AI poses to jobs.[6] The truth is, we're in the very early days of AI – sometimes it can be startlingly useful and then the next moment so strikingly terrible that it really is worse than useless. There are reasons to think that AI may always 'hallucinate', which is to say just invent untrue things. There are also reasons to think it may be possible to eventually make sure it doesn't do that. It is very engaging and interesting to speculate about what's going to happen, to experiment with the tools and see what conclusions you come to about what they can and cannot do. I think it's going to be enormous but, unlike with the internet at the time of writing this book, we're not *in the midst of it* yet. I'm certainly intending to keep updating my thoughts on this – and probably this book too – as we get inside the LLM information crisis.

Having said all of that, as I pointed out regarding Claude, in some ways we do know what's going to happen with AI because it's the same as what happened after the invention of cuneiform. More fear, more anger, more insults to various kings, more loneliness, more ability to replace other humans with technology. And fascinating opportunities. I recommend technologist and researcher Rachel Coldicutt's article on 'Responsible-ish GenAI dos and don'ts' for a gallop through thoughts about how to use this new technology.[7] For myself, I have found it much more use as a teacher than as a writer. It is brilliant when, for example, I upload a few paragraphs from a difficult article I'm reading and ask the AI to reword it in a simpler way, or when I'm practising French and want it to write me an article that is just challenging enough for my difficulty level. As I said in my novel *The Future*: books and printing can record thoughts, but machine learning records *ways of thinking*. I think it's going to be magnificently exciting, will let us do things we couldn't do before or do old things more quickly, and also will move us again away from Walter Ong's flexible, warm, human-centred world.

If nothing else, this book is an argument that once we do know the name of our epoch, we can work to look after ourselves and our societies and communities through it. Use the technologies for all the fascinating opportunities they offer. But also: have dinner with people in real life. Talk to real people not AI. Read a book over scrolling. Have the kind of hard conversation which builds relationships.

It's not my *favourite* thing to realize that I'm living through another information crisis. If I had a choice, I'd probably prefer to have been born in the dawning of another Enlightenment. But this is also a rare, once-in-several-centuries experience: to witness a new mode of thinking as it emerges. We get to see the egg crack. Actually, it's more than that: we get to feel our own minds crack open. Let's just try not to let it topple us into the kinds of madness that recur in information crises. No burnings at the stake. Just lighting more candles, driving away more darkness.

Notes

1. As a citizen of the UK, I want to acknowledge the extremely painful and complicated history in Northern Ireland.

    I don't come from Northern Ireland, but I do have family there. As someone who grew up in England I am *definitely* not the right person to say how the conflict in Northern Ireland should be defined, and certainly not that it's just 'between Catholics and Protestants'. The history and politics are much more complex than that.

    But I can't just blithely use the conflicts of the Reformation as an analogy for conflict in the modern world and suggest that somehow the Reformation conflicts are 'over' without acknowledging that this history plays a part in a painful situation in my own country.
2. It probably is just a legend. *The Cambridge Guide to Homer* (Pache, 2020) says: 'The matter of a "Pisistratean Recension", according to which the tyrant Pisistratus is credited with "assembling" Homeric poetry (here meaning exclusively the *Iliad* and the *Odyssey*), is troubling although a number of ancient sources refer to it as a fact.'
3. He wrote a book called *On the Jews and Their Lies*. Which I'm not proposing to direct you towards.

4 Vosoughi, Roy and Aral (2018):

> We investigated the differential diffusion of all of the verified true and false news stories distributed on Twitter from 2006 to 2017. The data comprise ~126,000 stories tweeted by ~3 million people more than 4.5 million times. We classified news as true or false using information from six independent fact-checking organizations that exhibited 95 to 98% agreement on the classifications. Falsehood diffused significantly farther, faster, deeper, and more broadly than the truth in all categories of information, and the effects were more pronounced for false political news than for false news about terrorism, natural disasters, science, urban legends, or financial information. We found that false news was more novel than true news, which suggests that people were more likely to share novel information. Whereas false stories inspired fear, disgust, and surprise in replies, true stories inspired anticipation, sadness, joy, and trust. Contrary to conventional wisdom, robots accelerated the spread of true and false news at the same rate, implying that false news spreads more than the truth because humans, not robots, are more likely to spread it.

5 Dodds (2019), 'We thought the internet would make a better world: Aza Raskin invented the infinite scroll, now he estimates it wastes 200,000 lifetimes a day':

One big regret is his invention of the infinite scroll (though others have also claimed credit). Once, long ago, internet users had to actually click 'next' when they got to the bottom of a web page. Mr Raskin, inspired by the smooth scrolling of Google Maps, fixed all that, making the page just load new content automatically like the magic porridge pot of lore. This feature was swiftly 'weaponized' to keep us endlessly refreshing our apps like gamblers desperately tugging the lever of a slot machine, and today Mr Raskin calculates, conservatively, that his invention wastes 200,000 human lifetimes every day.

6 Among many other useful things they say is this, which rather implies that the era of 'move fast and break things' does need to be over now if we'd rather that what we end up breaking isn't 'our entire global economy':

> I think a lot of work in the future will be working with sophisticated machines, but the people will still provide the glue, the supervision, the judgment, the decision making, and the context and contextual awareness that are so essential to making good choices, whether in medicine or law or education or skilled repair or replacing a water heater in a household. And I think there's enormous scope for people to be involved in that work. But if that all happened tomorrow, it would be a debacle, because many, many people's roles would all of a sudden be

redundant, and they wouldn't be prepared for what they're asked to do instead. If it happens over two decades, we have a much better chance of harnessing the productivity growth while making successful transitions. You know, there are many, many predictions that start with the sentence, AI will, AI will do this or will do that. I think it's important to recognise that AI will not do things on its own. It works for us and we have to decide what we want it to do. And that means setting the right priorities.

7 I especially liked this very sensible analysis:

> A lot of very literate and articulate people feel mortally offended by GenAI writing tools, but many people for whom those skills don't come so easily find those same tools to be very useful. Likewise, if you enjoy writing, it would be a great shame to routinely outsource that pleasure to a tool. There is no hard and fast rule here; while organisational, institutional, and governmental decisions about AI bring with them moral and ethical consequences, at an individual level making decisions about thriving, inclusion, and access come with a different set of considerations.

Bibliography

Books

Achebe, C., *No Longer at Ease*, London: Heinemann, 1960.

Assmann, J., *From Akhenaten to Moses: Ancient Egypt and Religious Change*, Cairo: American University in Cairo Press, 1997.

Barrett, D., *Supernormal Stimuli: How Primal Urges Overran Their Evolutionary Purpose*, New York and London: W. W. Norton & Company, 2010.

Baumann, G., *The Written Word: Literacy in Transition (Wolfson College Lectures 1985)*, Oxford: Oxford University Press, 1986.

Bellah, R. N. and Joas, H. (eds), *The Axial Age and Its Consequences*, Cambridge, MA: Belknap Press of Harvard University Press, 2012.

Beniger, J. R., *The Control Revolution: Technological and Economic Origins of the Information Society*, Cambridge, MA: Harvard University Press, 1986.

Blair, A. M., *Too Much to Know: Managing Scholarly Information before the Modern Age*, New Haven: Yale University Press, 2010.

Borges, J. L., *The Book of Sand*, translated by Norman Thomas di Giovanni, New York: E. P. Dutton, 1975.

Bowman, A. K. and Woolf, G. (eds), *Literacy and Power in the Ancient World*, Cambridge: Cambridge University Press, 1994.

Chiang, T., *The Truth of Fact, The Truth of Feeling*, Burton, MI: Subterranean Press, 2013.

Conger, K. and Mac, R., *Character Limit: How Twitter Rewrote the Rules of Communication and Changed Our World*, London: Penguin, 2024.

Cottret, B., *Calvin: A Biography*, Edinburgh: T&T Clark Ltd, 2000.

Eisenstein, E. L., *The Printing Revolution in Early Modern Europe*, 2nd edn, Cambridge: Cambridge University Press, 2005.

Encyclopedia Britannica, *100 Most Influential Scientists: Tycho Brahe (1546–1601)*, London: Constable & Robinson, 2008.

Graeber, D. and Wengrow, D., *The Dawn of Everything: A New History of Humanity*, London: Penguin, 2022.

Havelock, E. A., *The Muse Learns to Write: Reflections on Orality and Literacy from Antiquity to the Present*, New Haven: Yale University Press, 1986.

Holland, T., *Dominion: How the Christian Revolution Remade the World*, London: Little, Brown, 2019.

Jackson, T., *Postcard from the Past*, London: Fourth Estate, 2017.

Lanier, J., *Ten Arguments for Deleting Your Social Media Accounts Right Now*, London: Vintage, 2018.

MacCulloch, D., *Reformation: Europe's House Divided 1490–1700*, London: Allen Lane, 2003.

McLuhan, M., *The Gutenberg Galaxy: The Making of Typographic Man*, Toronto: University of Toronto Press, 2011.

Momigliano, A., *Alien Wisdom: The Limits of Hellenization*, Cambridge: Cambridge University Press, 1971.

Olson, D. R., *The World on Paper: The Conceptual and Cognitive Implications of Writing and Reading*, Cambridge: Cambridge University Press, 1994.

Ong, W. J., *Orality and Literacy: The Technologizing of the Word*, 2nd edn, London: Routledge, 2002.

Oppenheim, A. L., *Letters from Mesopotamia: Official, Business, and Private Letters on Clay Tablets from Two Millennia*, Chicago: University of Chicago Press, 1967.

Pache, C. O. (ed.), *The Cambridge Guide to Homer*, Cambridge: Cambridge University Press, 2020.

Postman, N., *Amusing Ourselves to Death: Public Discourse in the Age of Show Business*, London: Methuen Publishing, 1987.

Postman, N., *Technopoly: The Surrender of Culture to Technology*, London: Vintage, 1993.

Rounding, V., *The Burning Time: The Story of the Smithfield Martyrs*, London: Picador, 2017.

Singer, P., *The Expanding Circle: Ethics, Evolution, and Moral Progress*, Princeton: Princeton University Press, 1981.

Smith, L., *The Glossa Ordinaria: The Making of a Medieval Bible Commentary*, Leiden: Brill, 2009.

Stock, B., *The Implications of Literacy: Written Language and Models of Interpretation in the Eleventh and Twelfth Centuries*, Chichester: Princeton University Press, 1983.

Tinbergen, N., *The Herring Gull's World: A Study of the Social Behaviour of Birds*, London: Collins, 1953.

Wisnom, S., *The Library of Ancient Wisdom: How the Earliest Writers Recorded History*, London: Allen Lane, 2025.

Woolf, V., *Orlando: A Biography*, London: Hogarth Press, 1928.

Wynn-Williams, S., *Careless People*, London: Macmillan, 2025.

Articles and Online Sources
(all online sources accessed 16 May 2025)

BBC News (2024), 'Fact-checking RFK Jr's views on health policy', 15 November. Available at: https://www.bbc.co.uk/news/articles/c0mzk2y41zvo

Bellah, R. N. (2005), 'What is Axial about the Axial Age?', *European Journal of Sociology*, 46(1), pp. 69–89.

Bezos, J. (2025), [Twitter/X post about *Washington Post*], 26 February. Available at: https://x.com/JeffBezos/status/1894757287052362088

Booker Prize Foundation (2023), 'Generation TF: Who is really reading translated fiction in the UK?', 13 April. Available at: https://thebookerprizes.com/the-booker-library/features/generation-tf-who-is-really-reading-translated-fiction-in-the-uk

Cheadle, H. (2012), 'What is ASMR? That Good Tingly Feeling No One Can Explain', *Vice*, 31 July. Available at: https://www.vice.com/en/article/asmr-the-good-feeling-no-one-can-explain

Coldicutt, R. (2025), 'Responsible-ish GenAI dos and don'ts: text edition', Careful Industries, 1 April. Available at: https://www.careful.industries/blog/2025-4-responsible-ish-genai-dos-and-donts-text-edition

DemandSage (2024), 'Facebook Statistics'. Available at: https://www.demandsage.com/facebook-statistics

Department for Education (2023), 'School pupils and their characteristics: 2023/24', Explore Education Statistics. Available at: https://explore-education-statistics.service.gov.uk/find-statistics/school-pupils-and-their-characteristics/2023-24

Dodds, L. (2019), 'We thought the internet would make a better world: Aza Raskin invented the infinite scroll, now he estimates it wastes 200,000 lifetimes a day', *Daily Telegraph*, 10 May.

Gatehouse, G. (2021–25), *The Coming Storm* [podcast], BBC Radio 4. Available at: https://www.bbc.co.uk/programmes/m001324r

Gebru, T. (2023), 'Don't Fall for the AI Hype', interviewed by Paris Marx for *Tech Won't Save Us* [podcast], 19 January. Available at: https://podcasts.apple.com/us/podcast/dont-fall-for-the-ai-hype-w-timnit-gebru/id1507621076?i=1000595385583

Good Things Foundation (2024), 'Digital Exclusion in the UK'. Available at: https://www.goodthingsfoundation.org/policy-and-research/research-and-evidence/research-2024/digital-nation.html

Holland, T. and Sandbrook, D. (2020–25), *The Rest is History* [podcast], Goalhanger Podcasts. Available at: https://therestishistory.com/433-luther-the-man-who-changed-the-world-part-1

Meta Platforms, Inc. (2025), 'Quarterly Earnings Report', Meta Investor Relations, 29 January. Available at: https://investor.atmeta.com/investor-news/press-release-details/2025/Meta-Reports-Fourth-Quarter-and-Full-Year-2024-Results/default.aspx

Oxford Reference (2023), 'I would not open windows into men's souls', in *Oxford Dictionary of Quotations*. Available at: https://www-oxfordreference-com.libezproxy.open.ac.uk/display/10.1093/acref/9780191826719.001.0001/q-oro-ed4-00004114

PolitiFact (2025), 'Israel Fact-checks'. Available at: https://www.politifact.com/israel

Roose, K. (2024), 'How Claude Became Tech Insiders' Chatbot of Choice', *New York Times*, 13 December. Available at: https://www.nytimes.com/2024/12/13/technology/claude-ai-anthropic.html

Shannon, C. (2025), 'Do You Remember How Life Used to Feel?', Catherine Shannon's Substack, 27 February. Available at: https://catherineshannon.substack.com/p/do-you-remember-how-life-used-to-feel

Statista (2024), 'Facebook Products – statistics & facts'. Available at: https://www.statista.com/topics/751/facebook/#statisticChapter

Vosoughi, S., Roy, D. and Aral, S. (2018), 'The spread of true and false news online', *Science*, 359(6380), pp. 1146–51. DOI: 10.1126/science.aap9559

Wolf, M. and Autor, D. (2025), 'Martin Wolf talks to David Autor – could AI be a bigger threat to US jobs than China?', *The Economics Show* [podcast], *Financial Times*, 21 April. Available at: https://www.ft.com/content/4e260abd-2528-4d34-8fa4-a21eabfd6db9

Acknowledgements

This book started with a short piece by Walter Ong that I was set to read by the Open University for my MA in Classics, so thank you first of all to James Robson and the entire OU Classics department for setting me off on this journey. And thank you to Tom Holland who discussed the Reformation and the modern world with me on Twitter. Thank you to Jon Ronson, Adam Curtis and Annette Mees for enlightening conversations that shaped and pushed along my thinking. Thank you to Kara Swisher, for telling me the original idea was actually very smart.

Thank you to my father Professor Geoffrey Alderman who taught me to recognize that we are always living in history and that any news event can always be considered as the subject of future interesting PhDs.

Thank you to my friends Dr Benjamin Ellis, Esther, Russell, Daniella, Benjy and Zara Donoff. Very special thank you to Lorna, who has been through it with me.

Love, always, for OAD, DLA and SSA. Absolutely always.

Enormous thanks to Di Speirs of BBC Radio 4 who honed the original idea with me, edited multiple drafts of the radio essays and – very importantly – told me when what I was saying didn't really quite yet make sense, and to Richard Hamilton-Jones, particularly for reminding me about *Orlando*. Thanks to Mohit Bakaya who supported the idea from the start, to Hugh Levinson who commissioned the essays, and to Nicola Holloway who produced them. Extreme thanks to Greg Jenner who read the essays just before I recorded them to check for egregious historical errors. Any errors that remain are of course my own.

Thank you to my wonderful agent Veronique Baxter, to my brilliant assistant Niamh Cumming and to the amazing team at Penguin: Sarah-Jane Forder, Natalie Wall, Anna Lambert, Leah Boulton and the only editor I've ever left two publishing houses for, Helen Garnons-Williams.